NORWAY

Bladir

upang

SWEDEN

Birka

Gotland

DENMARK

Roskilde

Hedeby

Dvina

Neva

Volkhov

Novgorod

Lovat

BULGARS

Volga

Ural

Aral Sea

Baltic Sea

Daugava

KIEVAN
RUS

Cologne

Rhine

Elbe

Oder

Vistula

SLAVS

Cracow

Kiev

Dneiper

Dniester

Don

KHAZAR
KHANATE

Volga

Caspian Sea

CHINA

INDIA

PERSIA

EMPIRE

HUNGARY

PECHENEGS

Danube

Black Sea

Gorgan

PERSIA

Venice

Genoa

ITALIAN
STATES

Rome

SERBIA

BULGARIA

Adrianople

Constantinople

BYZANTINE EMPIRE

Mediterranean Sea

Jerusalem

Alexandria

ABBASID CALIPHATE

N
E
S
W

THE VIKING WARRIOR

THE VIKING WARRIOR

THE RAIDERS, PILLAGERS AND EXPLORERS WHO TERRORIZED MEDIEVAL EUROPE

BEN HUBBARD

amber
BOOKS

This edition first printed in 2018

First published in 2017

Published by Amber Books Ltd
United House
London N7 9DP
United Kingdom
www.amberbooks.co.uk
Instagram: amberbooksltd
Facebook: www.facebook.com/amberbooks
Twitter: @amberbooks

ISBN: 978-1-78274-738-3

Editor: Michael Spilling
Designer: Colin Fielder
Picture research: Terry Forshaw

Manufactured in China

Contents

Introduction

In 793 CE fierce omens were recorded in the skies over Northumbria: huge whirlwinds, lightning storms and reports of fiery dragons flying through the air. Then, on 8 June, a wave of Viking warriors broke with a terrible fury onto British shores. In a blizzard of sword blades and battle-axes, they attacked the Northumberland monastery of Lindisfarne and butchered the monks who lived there. Those not killed were carried away in chains; others drowned in the sea. With their ships laden with silver and ecclesiastical treasure, the warriors then set sail for home. The Viking Age had begun.

This is the popular perception of the Vikings, itself an evocative word that conjures up images of bearded warriors, shield-lined longships and piracy, pillage and slaughter. It is a description fed to readers in the West by medieval monks who sat scanning the horizon for striped sails and dragon-head prows with their nervous quills at the ready. For the monks, the Vikings were a thunderbolt from hell: they had appeared without warning and then went on to spread terror and ruin through Europe for almost 300 years.

Using their formidable longships the Vikings repeatedly raided the coastlines of Britain, France and Ireland; they sailed up river arteries to attack cities such as

Paris and London; they murdered, kidnapped and enslaved many thousands of people; and they plundered enough wealth to bring whole kingdoms to their knees.

Explorers in Search of Glory

But this is not the whole story of the Vikings, for behind the violence and destruction was a rich and complex culture created over many centuries in their homelands of Scandinavia. It was this culture that united the modern-day countries of Denmark, Norway and Sweden, and bound them by its customs, art, laws, language, stories and beliefs. Watching over the Vikings were their gods: the mighty Thor and the mysterious

Odin, the king of the gods whose ravens scoured the earth for news and fed on the corpses of the battlefield dead. It was these pagan deities that inspired the Vikings with their warrior spirit and sense of adventure. From childhood, Vikings were told to fill their lives with glory and honour, to seek wealth and fortune and to win long-lasting fame.

The greatest Vikings were immortalized in epic poems recited from one generation to the next; it was with these heroic tales ringing in their ears that young warriors went 'a Viking' abroad. But it was not all murder and mayhem: the Vikings also used their expert maritime skills to trade and establish new settlements in faraway lands. To enable this exploration and expansion, the Vikings developed the leading seagoing vessel of the medieval age: the longship. Powered by both oars and sails, Viking longships were swift, sleek and built with a shallow draught that allowed them to land quickly on shelving beaches and travel up rivers to ambush settlements inland.

The Vikings travelled extraordinary distances, reaching remote lands such as North America, unseen and previously undreamed-of by any European. But they did not only explore the waters of the North Atlantic – the Vikings also sailed east down the

Above: Viking descendants from the Shetland Islands celebrate the Up Helly Aa festival, which culminates in the burning of a replica longship.

Facing page: This Isle of Man runestone depicts Odin being devoured by the wolf Fenrir during Ragnarök, the last great battle of the gods.

Above: An artistic rendering of Eirik the Red (left), the legendary colonizer of Greenland, who is shown here fighting a duel in Iceland.

slaves in full public view, and sacrifice slave girls during boat burials for their noble dead. To the Arabs, the Vikings were unhygienic boors who carried out their morning ablutions in one shared washbowl. Alongside these warriors, described "as tall as palm trees and florid and ruddy of complexion", were their wives, who wore silver necklaces to show off their husbands' wealth. Unlike their hapless female slaves, Viking women were protected by the law and on a somewhat equal footing to men. It was illegal to force sex on a Viking woman, and any man who beat his wife would be hunted down like a dangerous animal.

Warrior Raiders

Violence, however, was only ever a moment away in the simple farming and fishing communities of Viking Scandinavia, and no-one was safe from the "berserkers". These were the semi-mythological warriors who would enter a frenzied state, foam at the mouth and attack anything that moved – friend, family or foe. Berserkers were the crack troops at the front line of any army abroad, but at home they were a blight on society; psychopaths who would rape and kill at will. As such, berserkers often wound up fighting other warriors in duels, a practice used to resolve disputes and restore honour.

Honour was of paramount importance to Viking warriors and offence was easily taken. Calling a warrior a woman or accusing him of being sodomized were terrible insults likely to result in duels. These were either impromptu

great rivers of Russia, to Turkey and the Caspian Sea. Many Vikings became regular traders in Constantinople, while at other times they simply attacked the mighty Byzantine capital. Some Vikings joined the ranks of the Byzantine emperor's bodyguard, the fabled Varangian Guard.

It is the Vikings in the east that we read about in astonished accounts by travelling Arabs. They tell us that the warriors would have sex with their female affairs fought to the death, or organized events conducted over an animal hide on an isolated island where nobody could escape. A duel, however, did not always heal an injury to a warrior's honour: the enmity could spill over into a generational blood feud that lasted until an entire Viking family had been wiped out.

A famous example was Eirik the Red, who had to flee Norway "because of some killings" and wound up in the Viking colony of Iceland. But trouble followed Eirik: he was soon tangled in two new blood feuds and in the end was banished from Iceland altogether. So Eirik set sail on the trackless sea and somehow landed in Greenland, where he founded a new colony. This was standard practice for Scandinavians during the Viking Age – there was often not enough arable land to go around and new farmland had to be sought abroad. When land was not readily available, it was simply taken.

The violent seizure of land also extended to nationwide conquest and invasion. For decades, the kings of Europe were forced to pay off their Viking attackers rather than suffer another round of raids. Appeasement did not bring a lasting peace. In 1013 CE, a vast Viking army invaded the battered English kingdom and installed Svein Forkbeard on the throne. It was a seminal moment that underlined the Vikings' ferocity and battle-prowess, and symbolized the high-water mark of their power. However, almost nothing survived of the Vikings' foreign realms.

Land was retaken, colonies were abandoned and Viking emigrants became assimilated into the local population.

But for the Vikings impermanence was at the heart of their worldview: life was about the here and now; everybody and everything was destined to die or go up in flames. This fatalistic outlook was supported by the Viking myth about the end of the world. At that time, the sun would grow dark, the stars would fall from the sky, the land would sink into the sea and the gods would destroy each other in a last battle known as Ragnarök. For the Vikings, their fate was sealed. All they had to do on Earth was create a lasting reputation and immortalize themselves in a great story. This is that story.

Above: A memorial stone to Eirik the Red's 982 CE landing in Greenland. The name was enough to convince many Icelanders to help Eirik colonize the new land.

Viking Origins

The sudden and violent Viking raid on the monastery of Lindisfarne in 793 CE struck Christian Britain like a thunderbolt. But desecrating the house of God and slaughtering unarmed monks meant little to the pagan warriors who believed in an afterlife of feasting and fighting in Odin's great hall. Nor were the Vikings and their beliefs anything new. Instead they made up part of a centuries-old culture formed far from view in the cold lands of the north.

The story of the Vikings is one of the people's relationship with the land and sea, and their isolation from the rest of Europe. From the time of Scandinavia's prehistoric period through to the eighth century CE, generations of proto-Vikings laid the cultural foundations for the raiders, traders and settlers we know as the Vikings today. They did so unheeded and largely unseen by the civilizations

Left: Stones shaped into the outline of ships mark out burial sites in the great necropolis of Lindholm Høje, Jutland, Denmark. The outlines represent the importance of ships in Viking society, not only in life but also in death.

Below: Boats shaped like Viking longships are among the thousands of rock carvings discovered at Alta, Norway. Dating to between 5000 BCE and 200 BCE, the artworks were created by the first known inhabitants of Scandinavia.

that came and went on the European continent.

Early Inhabitants

The first people to inhabit the Viking homelands of Norway, Sweden and Denmark were hunters and gatherers who emerged at the end of the last Ice Age. As the ice sheets retreated north these prehistoric people followed, fanning out across southern Scandinavia and settling in fertile regions such as Skåne in Sweden. Their preferred mode of transport was simple wooden boats, made watertight with animal hides and rowed with oars. The sea has always been central to life in Scandinavia, and it is no surprise that its first inhabitants were great mariners and boat-builders. They were also proud of their seafaring accomplishments, and made

pictorial records of their vessels in ancient rock carvings. The images connect these early people with another great Scandinavian tradition: fighting and raiding. Rock carvings dating from around 1100 bce in Sweden and Norway depict boats with a similar shape to the Viking longships that would follow 2000 years later; aboard them are passengers carrying axes and bows and arrows.

On land, Scandinavia's technology followed a similar path to the rest of Europe: agriculture was practised from around 4000 BCE; the Bronze Age emerged in around 2000 BCE; and the Iron Age began around 500 BCE. Little is known about the Scandinavian people during this time, although evidence of a few small farming settlements has been found, as have the human victims of

Above: Many of the Bronze Age rock carvings found at Tanum, Sweden, feature warriors aboard boats holding weapons. Many of the boats resemble the Hjortspring Boat, an early vessel used for war.

Facing page: An army of proto-Vikings are shown defeating the Roman legions in this painting of the Battle of the Teutoburg Forest. The winged helmets are an anachronistic embellishment.

sacrifice, preserved through the ages in peat bogs. More is known about Scandinavian society from the onset of the Imperial Roman Empire. From the first century CE, goods such as amber were traded south to the Roman Mediterranean, and Iron Age weapons made their way north in exchange. This was a dangerous, violent and uncertain time in Scandinavia, where hill

The Hjortspring Boat

The Hjortspring Boat is Europe's oldest plank vessel and a splendid example of the early boat-building skills of the Viking ancestors. The remains of the 18m- (59ft-) long vessels have many of the features associated with the streamlined Viking longships that were to follow. It is made of a "clinker" construction, with overlapping planks, or "strakes", along the sides that meet at each end of the boat. The ends formed into prows – one at each end, so the boat could make a quick getaway after being beached, which was also an important feature of the Viking longships. Also, like its Viking successors, the Hjortspring Boat featured a shallow hull that enabled beach landings and travel in estuaries and rivers. The boat was propelled by 24 oarsmen, with space for two navigational oarsmen at either end. The burial of the Hjortspring Boat in a bog may have been to give thanks or to honour the dead who had fallen in battle.

Above: The remains of the canoe-shaped Hjortspring Boat, which was buried with a cache of weapons.

Facing page: The reconstructed fort of Eketorp on the island of Öland, Sweden. First built around 400 CE, the fort was mysteriously abandoned in 600 CE.

forts were built to protect local inhabitants and large caches of weapons were cast into bogs as sacrifices, most notably in the northeast of Denmark's Jutland. By now, the practice of votive offerings was already hundreds of years old. One famous example is the Hjortspring Boat, buried as a sacrifice in around 350 BCE. The large number of weapons and armour onboard suggests wars between Scandinavian tribes were already in full swing.

On the Viking Brink

The cultural and political developments in Scandinavia took place far from the influence of Europe's first great superpower – Rome. Rome was the civilization that dominated the rest of Europe during the Iron Age and up until the fifth century CE, but it never came close to conquering Scandinavia. The Roman historian Tacitus tells us that Roman ships were sent by Augustus in 5 CE to explore the land around Denmark, although it is unclear if the legionaries landed. It was the only attempt at a Roman incursion by sea, which produced little more than the name "Scandinavia", a derivation of "Scadinavia" or "the dangerous island". Any Roman attempts to reach Scandinavia by land were thwarted by the

massacre of three of its legions during the 9 CE Battle of the Teutoburg Forest. This humiliating defeat ended any further Roman forays east of the Rhine, and Scandinavia's most southerly border along Denmark's Eider River was certainly never troubled.

The Battle of the Teutoburg Forest was an unprecedented moment for Rome, the civilization that went on to conquer two-thirds of the known world and create an empire that stretched for over 4 million square km (2.5 million square miles). Every new territory that fell under the Roman legions was quickly turned into a little Rome, as

foreign towns and cities were fitted with modern aqueducts, roads, baths and amphitheatres, and ruled by a written law. By spreading the latest in modern infrastructure, technology and literacy to the territories of Europe the Roman Empire brought an end to the prehistory of many of its tribal peoples. But none of Rome's "civilizing" benefits were experienced by the tribes of Denmark, Norway and Sweden. Nor was Scandinavia affected by the Migration Period between 400 and 600 CE, which spelled the end of Rome's domination and dislocated large sections of the European population. During this

time, Angles and Saxons invaded England, Rome was overrun by Visigoths and Christianity began to make its mark across Europe. The Viking ancestors had interactions with all of these people, to be sure, but their own cultural identity was formed entirely in isolation, away from any continental interference.

At the time of Europe's Migration Period, Scandinavia stood on the brink of the Viking Age. There were many different Scandinavian tribes during this period, although the people as a whole had many cultural elements in common. They all generally lived in small rural settlements

where they farmed, fished and, at times, fought one another. Before long, many of these settlements became fortified local centres of power as the regions of Scandinavia became organized into chiefdoms. One such centre was Eketorp on the Swedish island of Öland; another was at Gamla Uppsala in Sweden's Uppland. Founded in the third century ce, Gamla Uppsala was an important economic, religious and political centre before, during and after the Viking Age proper. The great burial mounds constructed for members of the Yngling dynasty at Gamla Uppsala can still be seen today and are of great archeological significance: they symbolize Scandinavia's evolution from a population made up of small tribes to regions ruled by kings.

During the final part of the Scandinavian Iron Age, known as the Vendel Period (600–800 CE), lavish burials also took place north of Gamla Uppsala at Valsgärde and Vendel. Here, kings were buried aboard their ships along with fine objects and weapons, a signature of their wealth, power and warrior spirit. This tradition of ship burials continued into the Viking Age.

As we have seen, even the earliest Scandinavian settlers were great ship-builders and sea-farers. Sea voyages were essential to travel around Scandinavia, and the waters around its fjords, inlets and islands served as the major transport arteries, replacing the need for longer and more perilous journeys by land. The Scandinavians' early maritime prowess showed itself in the daring and dangerous overseas

Above: Viking longships are pictured here travelling through the calm waters of a Norwegian fjord.

raids that gave the Vikings their fearsome reputation. But while the history of the early Scandinavian people was dominated by the sea, it was the land, with its vast and varied geography, that would shape the people of each of its countries.

THE HOMELAND COUNTRIES

The countries of Scandinavia – Denmark, Norway and Sweden – were not clearly defined territories with strictly controlled borders during the Viking Age, but they did make up the three basic areas of the Viking homeland. Scandinavia has experienced some small changes between the time of

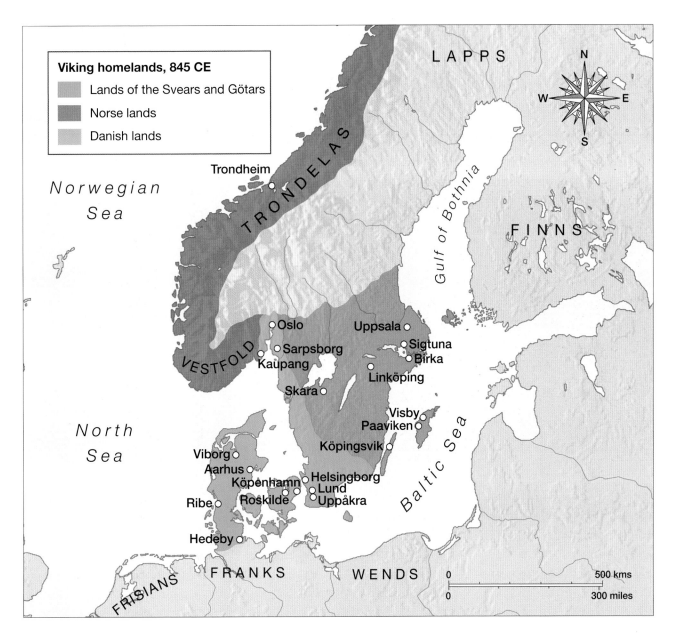

Viking homelands, 845 CE

- Lands of the Svears and Götars
- Norse lands
- Danish lands

Norwegian Sea

LAPPS

Gulf of Bothnia

FINNS

Trondheim

TRONDELAS

North Sea

VESTFOLD

Oslo
Sarpsborg
Kaupang
Uppsala
Sigtuna
Birka
Linköping
Skara

Visby
Paaviken
Köpingsvik

Baltic Sea

Viborg
Aarhus
Köpenhamn
Roskilde
Helsingborg
Lund
Uppåkra
Ribe

Hedeby

FRISIANS   FRANKS   WENDS

0   500 kms
0   300 miles

the proto-Vikings and the present day, such as reclaimed land and deforestation, but it is largely the vast and varied region it was for the first Bronze Age inhabitants.

Scandinavia is impressively long – it stretches for over 1931km (1200 miles) from the northern tip of Norway to Denmark's southern border along the Eider River – and it encompasses a wide range of landscapes and climates, from the freezing, forbidding north to the mild, fertile south.

At their northernmost reaches the countries of Sweden and Norway lie across the same latitude as Greenland and experience the seasonal extremes of the Arctic Circle. This means an average of only around one hour of daylight in mid-winter, but constant daylight during the middle of summer. Southern Sweden and Denmark, by contrast, lie on the same latitude as England, Scotland and northern Poland; the winters here are relatively mild and the summers warm. The Vikings and their ancestors had many cultural elements in common, but

Above: The Viking homelands as they looked after the Viking Age had begun. Although the territories are clearly marked here, borders between the three countries were often vague and volatile.

their ambitions and destinies were formed by the different regions they inhabited.

Norway

Norway is largely defined by its rugged coastline, one of the longest in the world at 18,000km (11,185 miles). Its coastal seaboard

Above: At 2469 metres (8100ft) above sea level, Galdhøpiggen is the highest mountain in Northern Europe. Norway's mountainous landscape often made journeys by sea an easier option for the Vikings than over land.

is protected from the Atlantic Ocean by long, snaking fjords and over 240,000 islands. Norwegian fjords can be up to 161km (100 miles) long, as is the case of the Sognefjord in western Norway, but seldom measure more than 5km (three miles) wide. During the Viking Age, the fjords provided safe passage for raiding longships sailing home to dock by the few strips of arable land suitable for

settlement. This land was mostly made up of small plains located at the neck of the fjords, where the rivers flowed down from the steep mountain plateaus above.

Overlooking its coast is the high, mountainous country that makes up most of Norway: 70 per cent of its landscape is rocky and barren and sits above the tree line, where Norway's coniferous forests cover about 25 per cent of the landscape. Much of the country's mountainous land belongs to the range known as the 'Keel', which runs roughly down the middle of the country and divides costal Norway in the west from its inland region in the east. The Keel has a permanent covering of ice and

snow and its highest point, Mount Galdhøpiggen – also Northern Europe's highest mountain – is 2469m (8100ft) above sea level.

Norway's fertile land makes up only around five per cent of the country's surface area and it is situated around the flatlands of Jæren, by the Oslo fjord in the southwest, and in the important Viking region of Trøndelag, south of the Trondheim fjord. The Vikings called their most northerly region Hålogaland: a strip of icy, sparsely populated land where tribes survived by fishing, hunting, trading in furs and taking tributes from the indigenous Saami people.

While life in the north was

tough, many of the other early Norwegians survived through a combination of animal husbandry, fishing, hunting and minor crop cultivation. The south was home to farming settlements and villages, and cattle and crops made up the mainstay of the local diet. Coastal dwellers supported themselves mostly through fishing and rearing a few animals. Norway's western coast is next to the Gulf Stream, so winters were mild enough for animals to be kept outside rather than sharing the longhouses as was the practice elsewhere. However, along the coast there was a limited amount of land, and it is little wonder that this region gave rise to the first Viking raiders of Britain. They were looking for new pastures abroad.

Among the country's resources Norwegian Vikings exploited for trade were animal furs, soapstone – used to make cooking pots – and bog-iron ore, which was extracted in large amounts from the Telemark province in the southeast.

> *"Craggy and barren, it is beset all around by cliffs, and the huge desolate boulders give it the aspect of a rugged and a gloomy land."*
>
> — *Saxo Grammaticus*

Sweden

Sweden is made up of a diverse interior, a coastline along its eastern, southern and southwestern sides, and a 1609km (1000 mile) western border with Norway; a divide made all but impassable by a long, high mountain range. In the north, these mountains are constantly covered with ice and snow, and their rivers feed the country's coastal plain in the east. These plains provide little in the way of arable land, but are instead covered by the coniferous forests that make up around 60 per cent of the country's landscape. Beyond the eastern plains, Sweden's coast

faces the Gulf of Bothnia and the western coast of Finland. Winters in this part of the country are particularly harsh and during the coldest time of the year the Gulf of Bothnia usually freezes over for months. The Viking inhabitants of this region survived by hunting, fishing and extracting iron ore for trade. To the north of the plains is the territory known as "Norrland", a cold and hostile place that even today is sparsely populated.

Central Sweden is made up of fertile lowlands around the lakes of Mälaren, Vänern and Vättern and below them the southern highlands and a low, unfertile plateau called "Småland". Småland

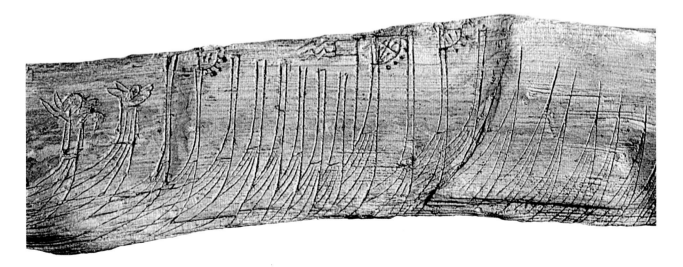

Above: A piece of wood discovered in Norway incised with an image of a fleet of Viking longships.

Above: The great royal burial mounds at Gamla Uppsala. An excavation of the western mound revealed the remains of a man alongside a Frankish sword, ivory chess pieces and cameos from the Middle East.

made a natural border between Viking Age Sweden in the north and Denmark in the south. Sweden's central lowlands were inhabited by two great Viking tribes: the Götar, who occupied the territory around Östergötland, Västergötland and Småland; and the Svear, who controlled the province of Uppland and give their name to today's Swedes.

Lying east of Sweden's coastline are the islands Öland and Gotland, which were of particular importance during the Viking Age. Sweden's islands and its closeness to the waterways of continental

Europe made the country a great nation of traders. Some of the first recorded sightings of Vikings were Swedes, who, unlike their Norwegian neighbours, emerged as traders in the far-flung marketplaces of Russia and Constantinople, rather than the raiders of Britain. An Indian statue of Buddha found on the island of Helgö in Lake Mälaren indicates the surprising geographical range of the Swedish traders. The island was also once the site of a busy marketplace that sold jewellery made in nearby workshops.

Like Norway, Sweden's largest farming settlements were found in the low-lying plains in its south. The largest of these settlements, around Uppland and Västergötland, grew from a handful of individual farms into kingdoms during the Viking

Age. Here, the abundance of crops and grazing land kept the local inhabitants in a style of luxury also enjoyed by those living in the fertile lands of Denmark.

Denmark

Denmark is the smallest country in Scandinavia, made up of the peninsula of Jutland and 443 islands that surround it. If a circle were placed around Denmark and its territories its circumference would only be around 720km (460 miles); but despite its small size it was no less important to the Vikings than its counterparts Norway and Sweden to the north.

As well as its numerous islands, including the important Viking-Age Sjælland and Fyn, Denmark also occupied the provinces of Skåne, Halland and Blekinge in

Saxo's Scandinavia

Saxo Grammaticus (c. 1150–1220) was the author of the *Gesta Danorum*, or "The Story of the Danes", the first known history of the country. In the book's preface he describes the three countries of Viking Scandinavia:

"Denmark is cut in pieces by the intervening waves of ocean, and has but few portions of firm and continuous territory; these being divided by the mass of waters that break them up, in ways varying with the different angle of the bend of the sea. Of all these, Jutland, being the largest and first settled, holds the chief place in the Danish kingdom. It both lies fore-most and stretches furthest, reaching to the frontiers of Teutonland, from contact with which it is severed by the bed of the river Eyder. Northwards it swells somewhat in breadth, and runs out to the shore of the Noric Channel (Skagerrak). In this part is to be found the fjord called Liim, which is so full of fish that it seems to yield the natives as much food as the whole soil …

But this country, by its closeness of language as much as of position, includes Sweden and Norway … Of these two, Norway has been allotted by the choice of nature a forbidding rocky site. Craggy and barren, it is beset all around by cliffs, and the huge desolate boulders give it the aspect of a rugged and a gloomy land; in its furthest part the day-star is not hidden even by night; so that the sun, scorning the vicissitudes of day and night, ministers in unbroken presence an equal share of his radiance to either season … It should be known that on the east it is conterminous

Above: An original illustration from *The Story of the Danes* by Saxo Grammaticus.

with Sweden and Gothland, and is bounded on both sides by the waters of the neighbouring ocean. Also on the north it faces a region whose position and name are unknown, and which lacks all civilization, but teems with peoples of monstrous strangeness; and a vast interspace of flowing sea severs it from the portion of Norway opposite. This sea is found hazardous for navigation, and suffers few that venture thereon to return in peace …

Now Sweden faces Denmark and Norway on the west, but on the south and on much of its eastern side it is skirted by the ocean. Past this eastward is to be found a vast accumulation of motley barbarism."

– Saxo Grammaticus,
The Story of the Danes,
translated by Oliver Elton

the southern plains of Sweden. On Jutland, Denmark's southern border runs for 67km (42 miles) roughly alongside the River Eider and was protected from continental Europe during the Viking Age by earthworks known as the "Danevirke". A gap in the Danevirke gave Danish Vikings easy trading access to their southern neighbours, the Frisians, Saxons and Slavs, and the European influence of these people in the Viking world was felt more keenly in Denmark than in Norway and Sweden.

Unlike Norway and Sweden, Denmark is a flat country that sits less than 180m (590ft) above sea level. Its fertile plains meant agriculture was the main occupation of its Viking inhabitants, who also relied on bounteous hoards of fish to supplement their diet. The country's strategic position between the North Sea and the Baltic also gave Denmark control over many of the trading routes of the Viking Age. It was therefore able to generate great wealth through its own trading ports, such as Hedeby in the southeast.

An important archeological site that shows the prosperity of Denmark's fertile plains is Borum

"For nine days feasts and sacrifices of this kind are celebrated. Every day they sacrifice one human being in addition to other animals."

— *Adam of Bremen*

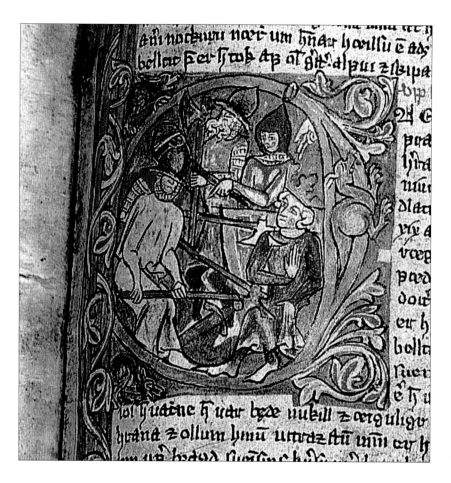

Above: An illustration from the Icelandic Saga of St Olaf. The sagas represent the first time Viking stories and poems were written down.

Eshøj, a settlement that included over 40 burial barrows dating as far back as 1350 BCE. A burial mound took over 100 people nearly three months to construct, and it was therefore an honour afforded only to the wealthy and powerful. Similar burial mounds found in Sweden's Gamla Uppsala, the site of the country's first kings, are further evidence of this theory.

RUNES AND SAGAS

For most of the Viking history before the eighth century CE, the bulk of our information comes from discoveries in archeological digs. During the time of the Vikings, and before them, little was written down. By sidestepping the influence of Rome, Scandinavia also missed out on one of the civilization's beneficial advances: the Latin alphabet. So Viking history and mythology were recorded in the oral tradition, usually through long poems passed from one generation to the next. The common language of the Vikings was Old Norse, also known as the "Danish tongue", which developed in the centuries leading up to the Viking Age and was spoken exclusively by the people of Denmark, Norway and Sweden, albeit with some regional dialectic differences. It was not until the Vikings' poems were compiled into the "sagas", penned from the thirteenth century onwards,

that Scandinavia had any kind of ordered written history. For this reason, the sagas were responsible for almost everything historians knew about the Vikings until modern archeology provided more clues. The sagas themselves are written with great poetic flourishes and warrior heroism in mind, so their historical accuracy cannot be taken too literally.

The Vikings, however, were not illiterate and they used a basic system of writing known as the runic alphabet. Originally created around 200 CE, this alphabet consisted of 16 letters made up of vertical and diagonal lines carved into wood, bone or stone. Horizontal lines were avoided as they could have been confused with the grain running along a piece of wood. Runic writing was not used to construct long rafts of text, but instead short sentences: an owner's name, a description of an object, a signpost, a magic inscription or a simple message or statement. Common runic script found on bone combs, jewellery or small pieces of wood contain messages such as "Thorfast made a good comb", "Melbrigda owns this brooch" and "kiss me".

Although runic writing was first developed to be carved onto pieces of wood and bone, runes were also used on metal and stone. Runic letters could be punched or incised onto metal and carved onto stone with a chisel and mallet. Large stones called runestones were commonly used to denote boundaries, roads and bridges, and also as memorials to the dead. Runic writing could be made more visible with a coat of red, black, brown and blue paint. The message was often embellished further by being decoratively carved along a shape, such as the outline of a serpent.

Hundreds of runestones have been discovered in Scandinavia and the Viking territories abroad, but their distribution seems unaccountably random. Over 200 runestones have been found in Denmark and several thousand in Sweden but only 40 have been found in Norway. The appearance of runestones in Viking territories is also oddly uneven. No

> ## *"Hákon raised these monuments in memory of Gunnarr, his son. He died in the west."*
>
> ### — *Swedish runestone*

runestones have been discovered in the Viking colony of Iceland, and only a handful found in Viking settlements of Britain. The Isle of Man, by contrast, has over 30 runestones with similar inscriptions to those found in Norway.

Memorial runestones from Scandinavia often stand as testimonies to Viking raiding activity abroad. The runestone dedicated to a Swedish man called Ali from Väsby records that he "took a payment of danegeld from

Above: Part of a tenth-century CE runestone found on the Isle of Man. The stone reports a Viking traitor: "Rosketil betrayed under trust a man bound to him by oath."

Right: The Swedish Kjula Runestone tells the story of the Viking Spjót, in poetic verse. Spjót, meaning "spear", was probably the name earned by the warrior in battle.

Cnut in England". Another rune-stone was erected by a Norwegian father for his son Bjor, who "met his death in the army when Cnut attacked England". A similar stone found on the Swedish island of Gotland reads: "Faðir had these runes cut in memory of Ôzurr, his brother, who died in the north on a Viking raid."

Runestones were often more than just a geographical marking post or a memorial to a warrior's passing. They also celebrated the virtues considered important to Viking society: valour, loyalty, honour, stoicism, honesty, generosity and heroism in battle – especially in death. Those who fought bravely and stood by their lords were often commemorated with a runestone. The great deeds of fallen warriors who died fighting in the face of overwhelming enemy numbers inspired whole poems rather than a couple of runic lines. One example is the Swedish Kjula Runestone, which was written in a poetic metre known as fornyrðislag, or "way of ancient words". Fornyrðislag was similar to the verse used in the collection of poems known as the *Poetic Edda* and the epic poem *Beowulf*. The Kjula Runestone reads: "Alríkr, Sigríðr's son, raised the stone in memory of his father Spjót, who had been in the west, broken down and fought in townships. He knew all the journey's fortresses."

The Kjula Runestone is famous among modern archeologists, not just because it was written in verse, but also because of its subject Spjót, which means "spear". Spjót must have been a powerful warrior to warrant a memorial runestone; it is thought his unusual name, almost certainly earned in the theatre of conflict, denotes a special prowess in battle.

Skaldic Poets

The *Poetic Edda* forms one of two main styles of Old Norse poetry: the other is the poetic tradition known as "skaldic". Skaldic derives from the word "skald", a poet who composed verse to describe current and historical events and the people involved in them. Viking-Age skalds often originally came from Iceland, but travelled extensively around

Scandinavia during their careers to visit the courts of kings. A skald who pleased a king could expect to be made a member of his court and would be required to compose a long poem in his employer's honour. Predictably, this would focus on the king's exploits and accomplishments and could later also be used as an oral obituary. Many of these poems have survived into the modern age after being quoted in the sagas.

One of the most important collections of sagas is a history of the kings of Norway called *Heimskringla*, written by thirteenth CE century Icelandic author Snorri Sturluson. In the preface to *Heimskringla*, Sturluson states the importance of the skaldic tradition in remembering the Viking kings:

"…we rest the foundations of our story principally upon the songs which were sung in the presence of the chiefs themselves or of their sons, and take all to be true that is found in such poems about their feats and battles: for although it be the fashion with skalds to praise most those in whose presence they are standing, yet no one would dare to relate to a chief what he, and all those who heard it, knew to be a false and imaginary, not a true account of his deeds; because that would be mockery, not praise."

– *Heimskringla*,
translated by Samuel Laing

The *Poetic Edda*

The *Poetic Edda* is a collection of 39 Old Norse poems compiled in Iceland in the thirteenth century. One of the longest poems is *Hávamál*, or "Words of the High One", a series of pithy maxims:

The man who stands at a strange threshold
Should be cautious before he cross it,
Glance this way and that:
Who knows beforehand what foes may sit
Awaiting him in the hall?

A guest should be courteous
When he comes to the table
And sit in wary silence,
His ears attentive, his eyes alert:
So he protects himself.

Drink your mead, but in moderation,
Talk sense or be silent:
No man is called discourteous who goes
To bed at an early hour.

The coward believes he will live forever
If he holds back in the battle,
But in old age he shall have no peace
Though spears have spared his limbs.

Foolish is he who frets at night,
And lies awake to worry.

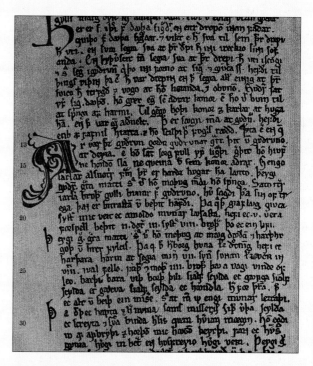

A weary man when morning comes,
He finds all as bad as before.

With presents friends should please each other,
With a shield or a costly coat:
Mutual giving makes for friendship,
So long as life goes well.

– *Poetic Edda*, translated by W.H. Auden & P.B. Taylor

It is difficult to believe a skaldic poet would be brave enough to actually scorn a Viking chief in his verses, whether it was true or not, but the information in the sagas does represent the Viking qualities thought most worthy of a wider audience.

In another section of Snorri Sturluson's *Heimskringla*, called the *Ynglinga Saga*, the author shows us how the sagas often crossed the line between mythology and historical fact. The Ynglings, one of the oldest known dynasties in Scandinavia, were based in Sweden's Uppland and were responsible for creating the great burial mounds at the settlement of Gamla Uppsala. The mounds were in all likelihood constructed for the three kings Aun, Egil and Athlis, who by all accounts were real people, although little is known about them. The factual basis for stories about several other kings, namely Domald, Eyestein and Swegde, is less clear, but the *Ynglinga Saga* doesn't let historical gaps get in the way of a good yarn.

According to the *Ynglinga Saga*, Domald ruled during a period

Above: A nineteenth-century woodcut of a Viking skald reciting verse to an enraptured crowd.

Facing Page: A statue of the great thirteenth century author, Snorri Sturluson, standing in his native Iceland.

of "great famine and distress" in Uppsala. To counter the mysterious phenomenon of their failing crops, Domald's people made multiple sacrifices of men and cattle over several seasons – but all in vain. As a last-ditch attempt, the people of Uppsala convened and decided that King Domald was to blame for the bad harvests, and to appease the gods, his head must roll. Domald was ambushed and murdered, and his blood sprinkled on the land:

> "It has happened oft ere now,
> That foeman's weapon has laid low
> The crowned head, where battle plain,
> Was miry red with the blood-rain.
> But Domald dies by bloody arms,
> Raised not by foes in war's alarms –
> Raised by his Swedish liegemen's hand,
> To bring good seasons to the land."
> – The Yn*glinga Saga*, translated by Samuel Laing

Another Uppsala king, Eystein, memorably nicknamed 'The Fart', ruled in the classic Viking tradition – by raiding his neighbours and killing their cattle. Unfortunately, one of the territories Eystein plundered belonged to a king called Skjold, who also happened to be a warlock. When Skjold saw Eystein's ships appearing on the horizon for another raid, he took off his cloak and blew into it. This caused a rogue wave that sprang up between Eystein's ship and one beside it, and knocked the king into the sea. His men later retrieved Eystein's body and a burial mound was built in his honour.

King Swegde was one of the earlier rulers of Uppsala, and his story concerns his obsession with searching for the god Odin. Odin was thought to dwell somewhere in the east, and early in his reign Swegde swore to find him. His subsequent journey lasted for five years and proved to be fruitless. After a hiatus, during which the king married and fathered a son, Swegde once again set out on his quest. On his travels, Swegde came across a "stone as big as a house", and decided to stop there for the night. After an evening of feasting and drinking, he noticed a dwarf

Above: An interpretive illustration of the Ynglings' great hall at Uppsala, which some believe may have been a pagan temple.

Facing page: A small bronze statuette of the god Frey. According to Saxo Grammaticus, Frey was the god who introduced the concept of human sacrifice to the Vikings.

sitting under the stone. The dwarf called to Swegde and his men, beckoning them to a doorway in the rock that he claimed led to the realm of Odin. Drunk enough to believe such a story, "Swegde ran into the stone, which instantly closed behind him, and Swegde never came back."

The story of Swegde is of particular importance because it introduces the god Odin into the realm of the Uppsala kings. Uppsala was one of the main pagan cult centres of Scandinavia and the site of pagan worship, pagan burials and pagan sacrifices. The Ynglings' great hall, which overlooked the three monumental burial mounds, is believed by some to have been a pagan temple. The mounds themselves were almost certainly made for the kings Aun, Egil and Athlis, but they were called Odin's

Howe, Thor's Howe and Frey's Howe.

It is perhaps no surprise that some of the sagas report that various Viking gods originally came from Uppsala. In his thirteenth-century work The Story of the Danes, Danish author Saxo Grammaticus tells us:

"At this time there was one Odin, who was credited over all Europe with the honour, which was false, of godhead, but used more continually to sojourn at Upsala; and in this spot, either from the sloth of the inhabitants or from its own pleasantness, he vouchsafed to dwell with somewhat especial constancy."

Saxo also says that Frey, who lived nearby, was the god who introduced the concept of human sacrifice to the Viking world:

"Frey, the regent of the gods, took

his abode not far from Upsala, where he exchanged for a ghastly and infamous sin-offering the old custom of prayer by sacrifice, which had been used by so many ages and generations. For he paid to the gods abominable offerings, by beginning to slaughter human victims."

– Saxo Grammaticus,
The Story of the Danes,
translated by Oliver Elton

Uppsala retained its place as a pagan stronghold until the twelfth century, and was one of the last Viking territories to convert to Christianity. Perhaps this is the reason that Christian chroniclers describing Uppsala are somewhat concerned with the lurid details of human sacrifice and the bloodthirsty antics of the gods who apparently originated there. However, their record is the best that we have of a rich belief system in the pagan gods who bequeathed to the Vikings their fearless warrior spirit. For although those who sought out the gods in life – such as the Uppsala King Swegde – would search in vain, any warrior who fought bravely according to the Viking virtues would be ensured a place among the gods in death.

THE GODS

Unlike Christianity, the Viking religion did not have set ideas about good and evil. Nor did it have a priesthood or churches. Instead, the worship of Vikings gods revolved around rituals, sacrifices and festivals that were probably instigated by the kings or local chiefs. The Vikings believed that their lives and those of their

"For he paid to the gods abominable offerings, by beginning to slaughter human victims."

— *Saxo Grammaticus*

Above: Carl Larsson's 1915 painting "Midvinterblot", or "Midwinter's Sacrifice", is a rendering of the sacrifice of the Yngling king, Domald. It remains a controversial and much debated artwork.

gods were subject to fate. Their mythology explained how the world was created and also how it would end at Ragnarök, or "The Fate of the Gods": an apocalyptic event that would destroy everything, including many of the gods.

The Vikings believed in two families of gods, the Æsir and the Vanir, who behaved like the mortals they ruled over and were responsible for every aspect of their daily lives. The Æsir, the larger family, was connected with war and power, whereas the smaller Vanir family was more associated with cultivation and fertility. In some stories the two heavenly factions warred against each other and then joined together

as one peaceful group. The Æsir lived in a place called Asgard, one of the nine worlds united by the giant tree Yggdrasil. Asgard was a green, fertile land that had an abundance of gold and jewels and was ruled over by Odin, the Æsir's father and chief.

Odin

Odin was the god of power, wisdom, poetry and battle, the oldest of all the gods, the creator of humans, and ruler of everything. He was a dark and dangerous god with supernatural abilities, including being able to change his shape and make a person lose their wits. From his throne in the great hall Valhöll, Odin could see across the known

Sacrifice At Uppsala

Adam of Bremen was an eleventh century author who wrote *Gesta Hammaburgensis ecclesiae pontificum*, or "The History of Hamburg's Bishops", a chronicle of northern Europe from 788 CE until his time. His text describes a temple at Uppsala that worshipped a trinity of gods that included Odin, Thor and Frey, and the ritual sacrifice that took place in their names in the nearby forest:

"A general festival for all the provinces of Sweden is customarily held at Uppsala every nine years. Participation in this festival is required of everyone. Kings and their subjects, collectively and individually, send their gifts to Uppsala, and, a thing more cruel than any punishment – those who have already adopted Christianity buy themselves out of these ceremonies. The sacrifice is as follows: of every kind of male creature, nine victims are offered. By the blood of these creatures it is the custom to appease the gods. Their bodies, moreover, are hanged in a grove which is adjacent to the temple. This grove is so sacred to the people that the separate trees in it are believed to be holy because of the death or putrefaction of the sacrificial victims. There even dogs and horses hang beside human beings. (A certain Christian told me that he had seen 72 of their bodies hanging up together.) The incantations, however, which are usually sung in the performance of a libation of this kind are numerous and disgraceful, and it is better not to speak of them."

– Adam of Bremen,
The History of Hamburg's Bishops,
translated by Francis J. Tschan

an eight-legged horse called Sleipnir.

Odin had several names such as "Helmeted One" and "God of the Hanged", and spent much of his time seeking wisdom and knowledge. This led him to the discovery of runes, which occurred on one occasion after he had ritually stabbed and hung himself from a tree:

> "I know that I hung on
> that windy tree
> For nine whole days and nights,
> stabbed with a spear, offered
> to Odin,
> myself given to myself
> high on that Tree
> whose roots no one knows.
> None refreshed me ever with
> food or drink,
> I peered down into the depths
> screaming aloud I grasped
> the Runes
> and then fell back from there."
> – *Poetic Edda*,
> translated by Olive Bray

Odin later gave the gift of poetry to men and sacrificed one of his eyes for a drink from the well of wisdom. His ongoing search for knowledge once saw Odin pitted against the giant Vafthruthnir, who had travelled all of the nine worlds and boasted that his knowledge was greater than anyone else's. Odin visited Vafthruthnir in disguise to challenge him to a game of wits, during which he learnt many of the world's secrets before defeating the giant with a trick question.

Odin was the most aristocratic of the gods and mainly worshipped by kings and chieftains. However, it was not Odin but his son Thor who was the most popular Viking god.

Above: A illustration of Yggdrasil, the "World Tree", which united the nine worlds, according to Viking mythology. The gods assembled at Yggdrasil for their daily "Thing", which were meetings held to discuss important issues.

world, aided by his two raven informers, Hugin (Mind) and Munin (Memory). Like all of Odin's wolves, the ravens were battlefield scavengers that fed on corpses. Odin was unpredictable in his ways and meted out life and death seemingly without reason. However, those Viking warriors who had fought bravely would be assured a place alongside Odin at Valhöll. He would fill their time with fighting and feasting, while they waited for Ragnarök and the last great battle of the world. Odin himself was a fierce warrior armed with a spear and rode

Below: The Tjängvide image stone from Gotland, Sweden, shows a dead warrior astride Odin's horse Sleipnir, accompanied by a Valkyrie who is offering a horn of ale.

Thor

Thor was considered the mightiest of the gods, and was a particular favourite among the common people of Scandinavia. He was a wild, red-eyed god, who rode a chariot pulled by two goats and wielded the mighty hammer Mjöllnir. As the god of thunder and lightning, Thor caused the skies and the earth to shake and crack as he rode across them. With Mjöllnir, Thor guarded the world against the giants, a menacing enemy who inhabited the outer reaches of the world. Thor had great physical strength and supernatural powers, but he also had a down-to-earth aspect and was considered solid and reliable. He controlled the weather and crops, and farmers would often make sacrifices to Thor by spilling the blood of animals over their soil. His hammer Mjöllnir represented fertility, and smaller versions worn as amulets and good luck charms have been found buried all over Scandinavia.

Thor's great popularity across the Viking homeland is still in evidence today: many things carry his name. These include the place names Thorsager (Thor's acre) in Denmark and the Thorshoftn headland in Iceland.

Facing page: A nineteenth-century painting of Thor fighting the giants with his mighty hammer Mjöllnir. Thor protected the world against the giants, who lived at its outer reaches.

Below: A tenth-century amulet of Thor's hammer Mjöllnir, found in Uppland, Sweden. Mjöllnir was powerful enough to level mountains, but it came with a flaw: a distinctly short handle.

The Thorbagge (Thor's bug) beetle was named after the god, as was the red Icelandic fox, Holtathórr (Thor of the holt). Images of the god carved onto runestones have also made their way through the ages. The eleventh century Altuna stone, found in Sweden, is of particular interest. This shows Thor in one of his most famous battles with his arch enemy, the Midgard Serpent, who could grow large enough to wrap his body around the earth and bite his own tail. On the Altuna stone, Thor is shown baiting his hook with the head of an ox to catch the Midgard Serpent. In the story, the Midgard Serpent was duly snagged on the hook and rose from the waves spitting poison and blood until Thor's fishing companion, Hymir the Giant, cut the line in fright.

After many more encounters, Thor and the Midgard Serpent fought in the last great battle of Ragnarök. At the end of their bout the Midgard Serpent was slain, but Thor found himself mortally wounded by the serpent's venom and fell down dead after taking nine steps forward. But not all of the stories concerning Thor were solemn and somber. In a more comedic poem from the *Poetic Edda* the giant Thrym steals Thor's hammer Mjöllnir and demands the goddess Freya's hand in marriage before it will be returned. In response, Thor dresses as Freya in a bridal costume and, with the god Loki in tow, thunders across the sky to the land of the giants. The giants seem wholly taken in by the disguise even when Thor displays such masculine behaviour as consuming a whole ox, eight salmon and a barrel of mead at the pre-wedding feast. Fortunately Loki is on hand to ease the giants' misgivings by explaining that the bride had not eaten for seven days because of her excitement at being wed. In the end, the giants hand over Mjöllnir as a wedding gift, whereupon Thor throws off his nuptial gown and proceeds to batter the giants, "and so Odin's son got his hammer back".

Other Deities

The Vikings worshipped many other gods besides Odin and Thor, including Odin's wife Frigga and his son Baldr, the gold-toothed Heimdall and the one-handed god of law, Tyr. Two of the more important deities were Frey and his sister Freya, originally from the Vanir family of the gods. Frey was a fertility god often depicted with a large, erect penis, who was thought to bestow "peace and pleasure on mortals". He also controlled the weather and "the fortunes of men". According to Adam of Bremen, Frey was born in Uppsala, but place-names and poems show he was worshipped across all of Scandinavia. Frey's sister was Freya, a feminine replica of her brother and leader of the *disir*, a race of female demigods associated with fertility in humans. According to the *Poetic Edda*, Freya claims half of the dead to join her in the afterworld, with the other half going to Odin. Other sources indicate that Freya only has jurisdiction over dead females.

In her capacity as a goddess of the dead, Freya is similar to the Valkyries, or "choosers of the slain". The Valkyries were demigods who did not belong to either the Æsir or Vanir families, but instead existed to pick the dead from the battlefield and welcome them to Valhöll. Late in the Viking Age, images of the Valkyries were toned down to depict them as Odin's robed assistants holding out horns of ale. But the earlier, unsanitized version portrays them as ghoulish demons who fed on battlefield carrion just like Odin's wolves and ravens. Verses from the skaldic

"Thor flashed fiery glances at the Serpent, and the Serpent in turn stared up toward him from below and blew venom."

— *Gylfaginning*

poem *Darraðarljóð*, found in the Icelandic *Njal's Saga*, gives this view of the Valkyries as vengeful harbingers of war and death:

"Blood rains from the
cloudy web
On the broad loom of slaughter
The web of man grey as armour
Is now being woven;
the Valkyries

Will cross it with a
crimson weft.

The warp is made of
human entrails;
Human heads are used as
heddle-weights;
The heddle rods are
blood-wet spears;
The shafts are iron-bound
and arrows are the shuttles.

With swords we will weave
this web of battle.

It is horrible now to
look around
As a blood-red cloud
darkens the sky
The heavens are stained
with the blood of men,
As the Valkyries sing their
song."

– *Njáls Saga*,
translated by
George W. Dasent

Alongside the Valkyries were
other deities not associated
with the Æsir or Vanir families,
but who played leading roles in
Viking mythology. Among them
were the goddesses of fate called
the "Norns", who ruled over the
destinies of mortals and other
gods. Inhabiting the human
world with the Vikings were the
dwarves, who lived in mainly
deserted places, and the elves, who
lived underground. Dwarves and
elves were among the supernatural
beings that humans needed to
please or appease in some way.

Like the pagan gods of other
civilizations, these deities often
required sacrifices or bargains
before they would grant human
wishes. However, no deal could
be made with the enemies of gods
and men, the giants, the god Loki
– father of the Midgard Serpent
– and the wolf Fenrir. It is Fenrir
who overcomes and kills Odin at
Ragnarök as the world comes
to an end. Losing their lives
alongside Odin are the gods
Thor, Tyr, Freya, Heimdall and
Loki, according to the *Poetic
Edda*, when: "The Sun grows
dark, Earth sinks into the sea, the
bright stars fall from the skies,
flames rage and fires leap high,
heaven itself is seared by heat."

The Hunninge Stone

Over 400 carved picture stones depicting Viking life and mythological figures have been found on the island of Gotland in Sweden. Among them is the three-metre (10-ft) high Hunninge Stone, which shows common Viking motifs: on the bottom panel, a farmer is sowing his crops; on the middle panel, the farmer goes off raiding in a Viking longship; on the top panel the farmer-warrior is transported to Valhöll by Odin's steed Sleipnir. But the stone is also thought to illustrate scenes from Atlakviða, a poem from the *Poetic Edda*. In the poem, King Atli invites King Gunnarr to his home, but then deceives and murders him by throwing him into a pit of snakes. Gunnarr's sister Guðrún then kills Atli, her husband.

Right: The top two panels of the Hunninge Stone showing the snake pit, the longship and the voyage to Valhöll.

Above: An Icelandic wood panel showing Odin being swallowed whole by the wolf Fenrir during Ragnarök – the end of the world.

Facing page: "The Ride of the Valkyries" by the English artist Arthur Rackham gives a storybook view of the "choosers of the slain".

> *"The Sun grows dark, Earth sinks into the sea, the bright stars fall from the skies."*
>
> — *Poetic Edda*

It is telling that the Viking gods themselves were doomed to die fighting like the worshippers they inspired. Both mortals and immortals, then, were predestined to follow a fatal path. In the end, the best that either could aspire to was the creation of a great legacy, as the poem *Hávamál* advises:

"Cattle die, kindred die,
Every man is mortal:
But I know one thing that never dies,
The glory of the great dead."

It is with this belief system in mind that the Viking raiders terrorized the shores of Christian Britain at the end of the eighth century. Being made to atone for a life of sin by one omnipotent god meant nothing to these pagan warriors, and nor did the concept of sin itself. Instead their gods encouraged them to fight, to conquer and to forge reputations as great warriors. Death was of little consequence to those who had Odin and Thor watching over them – as long it was an honourable death. To the Viking warriors, leaving a heroic legacy was what mattered most and to be remembered as a coward was the worst fate imaginable.

Viking Society

It is in death that the Vikings left telling evidence about their everyday lives, their social structure and the items most precious to them on earth. Great ship burials for important warriors reveal not only a wealth of artefacts and weapons but also clues about the hierarchy of Viking society. At the top was a king or earl, and at the bottom the slaves who could expect to be sacrificed to follow him to the afterlife.

I n Viking society a slave, or "thrall", had the same status as a domestic animal and usually slept in the dark end of a longhouse among the cattle. A Viking owner could treat his thrall in any manner he pleased and female thralls had to obey any sexual demand. A thrall who disobeyed or was considered not of use could be killed without legal repercussions.

Previous page - main image: A painting depicting a Viking funeral. When Vikings died in foreign countries, they were often buried aboard their ships which were then set alight.

Previous page - inset image: A ninth-century gold pendant discovered on the Swedish island of Gotland. Jewellery showed off a Viking wearer's wealth and could also be sold or bartered.

Thralls

Thralls were also one of the Vikings' most valuable commodities. Thousands were kidnapped from their native shores and shipped across vast trading networks stretching from Ireland in the west to Constantinople in the east. It was in the east, in a Viking trading settlement on the banks of the Volga River in modern-day Russia, that a rare account of Viking slaves was written. The author, Ibn Fadlan, was an Arabic diplomat who describes his contact with the Swedish Viking traders, known as the Rus, in 922:

> "They come from their own country, anchor their ships in the Volga, which is a great river, and build large wooden houses on its banks. In every house there live ten or twenty, more or fewer. Each man has a couch, where he sits with the beautiful girls he has for sale. Here he is as likely as not to enjoy one of them while a friend looks on. At times several of them will be thus engaged at the same moment, each in full view of the others. Now and again a merchant will resort to a house to purchase a girl, and find her master embracing her, and not giving over until he has fully had his will."
>
> – Ibn Fadlan's Account of Scandinavian Merchants on the Volga in 922, translated by A.S. Cook

Thralls were usually captured during raids or in warfare. Most would never see their homeland again, but Christians kidnapped in British raids were also held for ransom and returned if the right price was met. However, thralls were not only those who had been snatched and shipped off to sea: Vikings themselves could also end up as thralls. Certain crimes, such as murder and theft, could be punished with a sentence of slavery, and there is evidence of at least one woman forced to become the thrall of another that she stole from. Vikings who were unable to pay their debts or who had a choice of slavery or the death penalty could also become thralls. Other thralls were born to thrall parents and bound to live as slaves under the same owner.

Thralls represented a large chunk of Viking commerce abroad, but they also made up an important part of everyday life in Scandinavia. Thralls comprised around 25 per cent of the local Scandinavian population and it was considered normal to own one. The Viking "Frostathing law" of Norway suggests that three thralls was the correct average amount for a farm with a dozen or so head of cattle, whereas the estate of a noble required over 30.

In financial terms, thralls were worth about as much as the cattle they tended, but manual labour was not their only work. Many tilled the fields, while others tended to household chores, and a few worked as officials on large estates. Thralls were at times also sacrificed and buried with their owner, so they could follow him into the

Facing page: A Viking discusses the price of a slave with an Arab merchant. During the Viking Age, buyers in the east had an insatiable desire for female slaves from the west.

Below: Re-enactors go about daily life in a Viking camp in the Irish National Heritage Park, Wexford.

Above: Here, re-enactors play the part of "Karls", or free men, who represented the majority of men in Viking-Age Scandinavia.

Facing page: The remains of a Viking longhouse in the Shetlands, an archipelago 170km (105 miles) northeast of the British mainland.

afterlife and continue working for him there. Those thralls who no longer served a purpose on earth could be killed by their owner, in the same manner as a domesticated animal. While an owner was legally within his rights to murder his thralls, killing another owner's thrall was a crime that required compensation. The cost of a thrall differed from country to country, but in the slave markets of Dublin a female thrall could be bought for eight ounces of silver and a male for 12 ounces.

The lot of a Viking thrall depended entirely on his or her owner. There is evidence that some thralls were adopted into the family life of a particular Viking longhouse and lived a relatively comfortable existence. Thralls were also allowed to marry each other, although their children would be born as thralls. Some earned enough money to buy their freedom or were granted it by their owners. However, a slave had no property or rights, and if they attempted to escape they would

be hunted down and killed like a dangerous animal.

Thralls were on the bottom rung of the Viking social ladder that included free men above them and rulers at the top. The Vikings believed this three-tier class system had been divinely ordained, as described in the mythological tenth-century poem *Rígsþula*. According to *Rígsþula*, the god Rígr – another name for Heimdall – was responsible for creating the classes, and the first offspring from each one was given a name to distinguish them: Thrall (slave), Karl (free men) and Jarl (nobility). In the story, the thralls are described as disagreeably ugly and unrefined, and literally born to a life of servitude. By comparison, the Jarls at the top are beautiful, cultivated

and genteel. The Karls in the middle are industrious and capable, and in Viking Scandinavia the free made up the largest social group.

Karls

The free were the backbone of Scandinavian society. "Free" was also something of an umbrella term that included everyone from landless labourers and tenant farmers to large landowners who did not have noble status. Hunters and servants also fell into the free category, as did merchants and professional soldiers. There were three things that all free men held in common, regardless of their social standing or level of wealth: they were allowed to bear arms, they were protected by the law and they had the right to attend

and vote at "Things" – assemblies where lawsuits and disputes were heard and political decisions made.

However, Viking Scandinavia was far from an egalitarian culture, and there were different levels of status among the free. This was most apparent when compensation had to be made to a victim's family in the case of a murder or violent personal injury. If a murdered or injured man came from a wealthy or influential family, the size of the compensation payment would be markedly higher than if the man was poor. The rich were also more likely to receive compensation, as it was up to the parties involved to organize the payments. A wealthy landowner with warriors at his disposal had little problem collecting what was owed to him,

Rígsþula

The mythological poem *Rígsþula* tells the story of Rígr who visits three farms and in doing so fathers the three classes of mankind.

The first farm Rígr stays at is the home of a poor, elderly couple Ai and Edda (great grandmother and great grandfather). The couple feed Rígr coarse bread and at night he "lies in their bed between them". After three days he leaves. Nine months later, Edda gives birth to a son, Thrall (slave), who grows up well despite his unfortunate appearance: "With knuckles knotty and fingers thick; his face was ugly, his back was humpy, his heels were long." When he comes of age, Thrall meets the bandy-legged Thír (another name for slave), who is described as having "dirt on her sole, crooked her nose, her arm sunburnt." The two go on to have many children – the descendants of the Viking slaves – who live a life of hard labour and have names such as Badbreath, Horsefly, Stumpy, Fatty, Sluggard, Lout, Sticky, Roughneck, Ragged-hips, Bellows-nose and Beanpole.

Next, Rígr visits an orderly farm owned by a well-groomed couple, the grandmother Amma and the grandfather Afi. Afi is building a loom for Amma, who is spinning and weaving, and Rígr is able to give the couple good advice during his customary three-day stay. Amma gives birth to a boy called Karl (freeman, farmer), who has a ruddy-red face and sparkling eyes. As a man, Karl meets Snör (daughter-in-law, wife) and the couple have many children – the descendants of free men – with names such as Smith,

Above: In this detail from the Heimdall cross-slab at Jurby on the Isle of Man, the god Heimdall, or Rígr as he is also known, is depicted blowing the Gjallarhorn to signal the onset of Ragnarök.

Yeoman, Smoothbeard, Soldier, Lady, Bride, Sensible, Wise and Maiden.

Rígr's third visit is to a great hall owned by a finely dressed couple, the father, Faðir, and the mother, Móðir. The table is laid for him with bright linen, white bread, meat and wine, and the three stay up talking until the day's end. As usual, Rígr sleeps with the couple at night and once again sires a child, this time a son called Jarl (earl, warrior). Jarl is the early ancestor of the Viking aristocracy and has looks befitting his noble station: "Fair was his hair, bright his cheeks, his eyes as fierce and as piercing as a snake's." Jarl grows up, meets the slender-fingered Erna, and fathers 12 sons with regal sounding names: Son, Noble, Heir, Kinsman, Child, and Kon the Younger – a pun in old Norse that means king.

but this task was somewhat harder for a family of small means who could be easily intimidated.

Despite the apparent inequalities within the ranks of the free, Viking society was not socially static and it was possible to better one's position – or, indeed, make it decidedly worse. Becoming a Viking trader or raider were two ways of gaining fame and fortune. In the eighth century CE, all it took was a ship and a group of willing warriors to attack the coast of Britain and plunder at will. Those in Sweden could similarly become wealthy through the trading of thralls from the west and luxury items from the east. However, those who fell into debt by losing money they had borrowed against future successes could suffer the ultimate fall down the social scale: they could become a thrall.

Jarls

The most important members of the Viking nobility were known as "jarls", or earls. These were rulers of rank and influence who often rivalled the local regional king, if there was one. Jarls usually owned large tracts of land and held the principal seat of power in their region. They surrounded themselves with armed men and offered protection to local people in return for their political allegiance. A jarl was the leading voice at a Thing and took the role of arbitrator in legal disputes. Jarls also played an important part in times of war, by rallying men and building fortifications. Some jarls, such as Thorkell the Tall from Denmark, won enough wealth and

military experience from Viking raids to challenge the power of the king. For this reason each king trying to expand his territory and scope of control was often wholly dependent on the influence of the local jarls and counted on their support at the regional Things. To avoid this dependence, successful kings deprived the jarls of their authority and later incorporated them into their governments.

Kings

The system of kings in Viking-Age Scandinavia was confused and convoluted, and kings were rarely supreme national leaders. Instead, individual regions were ruled over by a series of kinglings who battled other petty kingdoms according to their divine ancestry and connection with an historic seat of power, such as Gamla Uppsala in Sweden.

To be in line for royal succession, a man could be descended from a king on either his mother's or father's side. This often resulted in multiple claimants for the throne at the end of a king's reign, and many long and bloodthirsty power struggles followed. Sometimes the outcome was the joint rule of a kingdom; at other times it meant civil war. The losers of these royal wars often went into exile overseas, sometimes to raid foreign shores with a boatload of battle-ready warriors. Sometimes these princely exiles stayed away permanently, content to set up a new kingdom in a different country. On other occasions, claimants to the throne returned to Scandinavia at the head of large armies to take their

"Fair was his hair, bright his cheeks, his eyes as fierce and as piercing as a snake's."

— *Rigspula* —

Above: A stylized image of Danish King Horik, who is shown here leading a raid. The horned helmet worn by the warrior on the left is a modern anachronism.

centres were established that brought in traffic from as far away as Dublin in the west to Constantinople in the east. The great number of valuable goods making their way across these trade routes and into Viking towns were prime targets for pirates, raiders and sometimes invaders looking for fast, easy loot.

Protector and Defender

To defend their towns, waters and business interests, the people of Scandinavia looked to a king who could provide them with protection, and this became the prerequisite for any heir seeking the throne. A king, therefore, needed to be backed by a large force of warriors who could be quickly assembled to defeat pirates, foreign enemies and opportunistic neighbours alike. He also needed to have links and peace agreements with other kingdoms, a sound administrative base and, of course, the blessings of the gods. Any aspiring king who could link his ancient ancestors to Odin, Thor or Frey was at a decided advantage. Finally, a king needed a vast amount of wealth to pay his warriors, build infrastructure and secure his powerbase.

A king charged with protecting the people of his own land often needed to raid the towns, villages and monasteries of foreign shores to keep his own coffers full. The amassing of silver, gold and expensive, glittering objects is one of the predominant themes of the Viking Age. Kings surrounded themselves with the treasures stolen from foreign shores and the exquisite jewellery crafted

heritage by force. Many kingdoms were in a constant state of flux until late in the Viking Age.

However, as the Viking Age wore on, the need for one all-powerful sovereign became more pressing. The period between 800 and 1100 CE was one of tremendous growth and wealth in Scandinavia, which in turn complicated the balance of Viking society. Much of this had to do with the great number of goods coming in and out of the Viking homelands. To support this exchange, towns and trading

in their own Viking workshops. Skalds (poets) who sat at the royal courts sang of great hoards of booty taken from raiding expeditions and the heroic deeds of the king's "félag" – a company of loyal warriors. In the king's hall his men and his fortune were on show for everyone to see, which was intended to both impress and intimidate.

It was not enough for a king to accumulate precious objects for his use only during his lifetime – he would also need them in the afterlife. The Viking nobility was buried with a treasure trove of items that included ships, sleds, weapons, wagons, household utensils, jewellery, food and clothes. Often these items were laid out alongside the king aboard his ship, which,

after an elaborate funeral ceremony, was buried under a large mound. The ceremony had a dual purpose: to send off the king in the manner befitting his royal station, and also to dazzle those attending with the wealth and luxury belonging only to society's most powerful members. Great funerals of the aristocracy lasted a long time in the memories of their subjects; they also gave those family members left on earth great status by association.

The remains of two large, aristocratic Viking funerals have been unearthed in modern times. In both cases the dead were buried aboard large seagoing vessels, known today as the "Oseberg Ship" and the "Gokstad Ship", discovered in Norway's Vestfold region. Dating to around 890, the

Above: Silver objects from the Cuerdale Hoard, a find of over 8600 items unearthed in Lancashire, England. It is the largest Viking hoard discovered outside Russia.

Above: A runestone from Gotland, Sweden, depicts a funeral procession to Valhöll. The rings the figures are carrying are thought to symbolise victory in battle.

Facing page: The Oseberg Ship, shown here, was used for the burial of two women in 834. One of the women is believed to be Queen Åsa of the Yngling dynasty.

Gokstad Ship probably belonged to King Olaf Gudrødsson of the Yngling dynasty, who was buried on its deck inside a purpose-built wooden burial chamber. Around the body were the objects not stolen by ancient tomb robbers – fishhooks, kitchen utensils and a game board. Also onboard were the skeletons of 12 horses, eight dogs, two peacocks and two goshawks. The sacrifice of animals and humans was not uncommon at the funerals of high-ranking members of the aristocracy. This practice, alongside the tradition of ship burials, was also not only limited to funerals held in Scandinavia – it was a custom that the Vikings took with them wherever they went.

An account of a funeral ceremony aboard a ship was recorded by Arab diplomat Ibn Fadlan, following his contact with the Vikings known as the "Rus" along the Volga River. The ceremony was clearly designed to impress onlookers such as Ibn Fadlan, whose blow-by-blow account also describes the sacrifice of a female thrall:

"When a great personage dies, the people of his family ask his slaves, 'Who among you will die with him?' One answers, 'I'. Once she has said that, the thing is obligatory: there is no backing out of it. Usually it is one of the girl slaves who does this. The tenth day, having drawn the ship up onto the river bank, they guarded it. In the middle of the ship they prepared a pavilion of

The Oseberg Ship Burial

Above: This wooden burial chamber, built on the Oseberg Ship's deck, served as the final resting place for the deceased women.

The Oseberg Ship was buried in 834 with two deceased women laid out on a raised bed in a tent-like wooden burial chamber behind the ship's mast. The chamber was decorated with ornately woven tapestries and contained a number of burial items alongside the dead. These included combs, clothes, sleds, wooden chests, agricultural tools, kitchen utensils, food, beds, a complete wooden cart and a bucket featuring a figure believed to be carved in the likeness of Buddha. The skeletons of two oxen, 15 horses and six dogs were also discovered. The women were of different ages and classes. One was aged 80, bore the remnants of fine, aristocratic clothes and is believed by some to be Queen Åsa of the Yngling dynasty, mother to Halfdan the Black and grandmother to Harald Fairhair. The other woman was around 50, and was not dressed in the same finery as her older companion. One study of her remains points to an Iranian birth, giving credence to other theories that she was a thrall sacrificed to follow the older woman into the afterlife.

wood and covered this with various sorts of fabrics. Then they brought a couch and put it on the ship and covered it with a mattress of Byzantine brocade. Then came an old woman who has charge of the clothes-making and arranging all things, and it is she who kills the girl slave.

"Then they took out the dead man clad in the garments in which he had died. I saw that he had grown black from the cold of the country. They put intoxicating drink, fruit and a stringed instrument with him. The dead man did not smell bad, and only his colour had changed. They dressed him

"The dead man did not smell bad, and only his colour had changed."

— Ibn Fadlan

in trousers, stockings, boots, a tunic and kaftan of brocade with gold buttons. Then they carried him into the pavilion on the ship. They seated him on the mattress and propped him up with cushions. Then they brought his weapons and placed them by his side. Then they took two horses, ran them until they sweated, then cut them to pieces with a sword and put them in the ship. The girl slave

who wished to be killed went here and there and into each of their tents, and the master of each tent had sexual intercourse with her and said, 'Tell your lord I have done this out of love for him.'

"After that the girl mounts onto the ship. The men came with shields and sticks. She was given a cup of intoxicating drink; she sang at taking it and drank. Then she was given

Above: Warriors push a burial longship out to sea as it is engulfed in flames.

another cup; she took it and sang for a long time while the old woman incited her to drink up and go into the pavilion where her master lay. Then the old woman seized her head and made her enter the pavilion and entered with her. Thereupon the men began to strike with the sticks on the shields so that her cries could not be heard. Then six men went into the pavilion and each had intercourse with the girl. Then they laid her at the side of her master; two held her feet and two her hands; the old woman looped a cord around her neck and gave the crossed ends to the two men for them to pull. Then she approached with a broad-bladed dagger, which she plunged between her ribs repeatedly, and the men strangled her with the cord until she was dead."

– Ibn Fadlan, *Risala*, compiled from translations by A.S. Cook and H.M. Smyser

THE PEOPLE

Anthropological studies of the skeletons found in Viking graves have shown what the people looked like in life. On average, the men were slightly shorter than Scandinavian men are today, with the average Viking male nearly 1.72m (5ft 8in) tall and Viking women around 1.57m (5ft 2in). However, those found in richer burial grounds were often considerably taller, and in some cases reached 1.87m (6ft 2in), a result of their better living conditions. An example is a grave in Langeland, Denmark, where a thrall had been bound, beheaded and buried with his owner. The thrall measured only 1.70m (5ft 7in) tall, while his owner was 1.77m (5ft 10in).

All Vikings, rich or poor, had badly worn-down teeth. This was due not only to the absence of regular brushing, but also the coarse bread that was a staple of their diet. Another common ailment revealed in the bones of Viking skeletons was osteoarthritis, and also the nicks and cuts created by deep sword wounds. Despite the hazards of their age, people of Viking Scandinavia lived relatively long lives compared with other Europeans of the period. Of those who grew to adulthood, around half could expect to live to 35, while the other half could reach 55 or sometimes older.

Below: The runestone of Harald Bluetooth who united Denmark and fortified its borders. Harald was later deposed by his son Svein Forkbeard.

A Brief History of the Kings

The histories of the Scandinavian kings are complicated and obscured by time and a lack of written evidence. Often a king ruled over some or all of one of the Viking homeland countries, and at other times they crossed the borders of Scandinavia to rule elsewhere.

Left: An illustration of Cnut the Great, or Canute, as he is otherwise known.

Denmark

The first Danish king we know by name was Godfred, whose kingdom in around 805 CE included all of Jutland, part of northern Germany, and the Swedish provinces of Skåne and Halland. Godfred was a warmonger who strengthened the Danevirke fortification along the border with Germany, but was murdered by his own people in 810. Godfred was succeeded by his nephew Hemming, but the throne was taken by Godfred's sons in 813. Godfred's kin retained power for many years until the last king in his dynasty, Horik, was overthrown in 853 by a family-staged coup.

From the mid-tenth century, there was line of Danish kings that included Gorm the Old and his son Harald Bluetooth, who united Denmark, ruled over part of Norway and built great fortresses around the Danish borders. In 987, Harald was deposed by his son Svein Forkbeard, a Viking who led many raids to raise capital against his rivals, the jarls Olaf Tryggvason and Thorkell the Tall. Svein Forkbeard went on to invade England in 1013.

Norway

Norway was divided into many petty kingdoms until 880 when the king of Vestfold, Harald Finehair, unified most of the country. Harald was succeeded by his son Erik Bloodaxe, but Erik was quickly ousted and went on to become a fearsome raider and later the King of York. Erik's successor was Haakon the Good, who stayed in power with the help of the powerful jarl Sigurd Håkonsson, but was later murdered by Erik's son Harald Greycloak. Harald was killed in a battle in 970 by an allied army of Danes and Sigurd's son, Haakon Sigurdsson. Haakon then submitted to the rule of the Dane, Harald Bluetooth, who was in turn overthrown by Olaf Tryggvason, the Norwegian Viking raider returning with great wealth from abroad. Olaf ruled for five years but was killed in the Battle of Svold by Svein Forkbeard and the jarl Eric Haakonsson, who divided rule of the country between them. Haakonsson later became the jarl of Northumbria under Cnut the Great.

In 1015, the raider Olaf Haraldsson became king of Norway but was deposed by Cnut the Great in 1028. Cnut was succeeded by his son Svein, who was in turn dethroned by Olaf's son Magnus. Magnus' half brother Harald Hardrada took sole rule of the country in 1047, but was later killed by King Harold Godwinsson at the 1066 Battle of Stamford Bridge.

Sweden

Little is know about the kings of Sweden during the Viking Age, apart from the stories surrounding the Yngling Dynasty at Gamla Uppsala, which are shrouded in mystery and mythology. We do know that the two main tribes of Sweden were the Svear and the Götar, and both were ruled by King Olof Skötkonung in the early eleventh century. However, neither Olof nor his two sons, Anund Jakob and Emund Slemme, were able to unite Sweden as a whole. They were also unable to convert Sweden into a Christian country, although they practised the religion themselves. Sweden remained the last bastion of paganism in Scandinavia until the twelfth century, when the country was finally unified as a Christian kingdom.

Left: The skeleton of a Viking warrior discovered in a pagan burial site. His final resting place today is the National Museum of Iceland, Reykjavik.

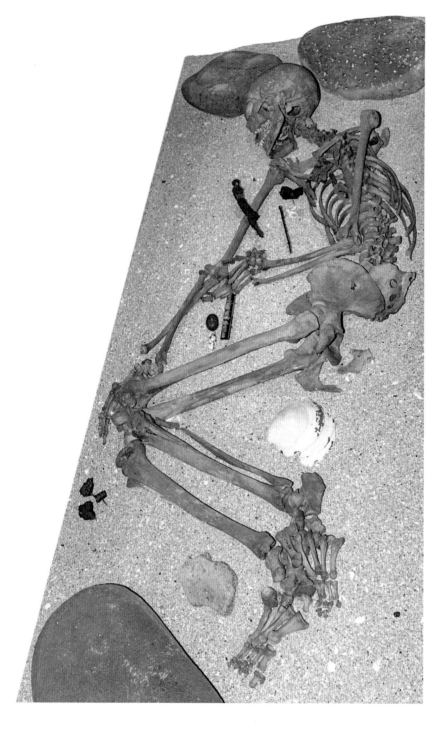

There are few pictorial images of the Vikings, but reconstructions of their skulls show there were less physical differences between the faces of men and women than there are in modern Scandinavians. Women's faces were more masculine than they are today, with more pronounced jawbones and eyebrows, and men's more feminine. These similarities in the features have often caused scientists difficulty in determining the gender of Viking skulls. The Vikings also sported the full range of hair colours – blond, brunettes and redheads – although there were a larger proportion of redheads in western Scandinavian and more blonds in the east. The stereotype of the blond, blue-eyed Viking from Sweden tallies with Ibn Fadlan's account of the Rus:

"I saw how the Northmen had arrived with their wares, and pitched their camp beside the Volga. Never did I see people so gigantic; they are tall as palm trees and florid and ruddy of complexion. Every one carries an axe, a dagger and a sword, and without these weapons they are never seen. Their swords are broad, with wavy lines, and of Frankish make. From the tip of the fingernails to the neck, each of them is tattooed with pictures of trees, living beings and other things. The women carry fastened to their breast a little

"Never did I see people so gigantic; they are tall as palm trees and florid and ruddy of complexion."

— *Ibn Fadlan*

case of iron, copper, silver or gold, according to the wealth of their husbands. Fastened to this case they wear a ring and upon that a dagger."

– Ibn Fadlan's Account of Scandinavian Merchants on the Volga in 922, translated by A.S. Cook

Clothing

Only a few images have been found of Viking women. The rare examples include gold and silver statuettes discovered in a Swedish grave and depictions of women on a tapestry from the Oseberg Ship burial. In both cases, the Viking women are shown with their hair tied up in a knot and wearing long gowns. While images are scarce, fragments of the actual clothes women and men wore have been found. Brooches discovered on Viking skeletons have at times revealed the imprints of fabric, or

have even trapped and protected a scrap of cloth from the eroding elements. Sometimes old clothes were used as tarring brushes, and the material was preserved within the tar for future generations.

Most Viking clothing was made of wool and linen and sometimes rarer, exotic cloth, such as silk from the east. While silk was reserved only for the rich, fur – used in Viking cloaks – was abundant in Scandinavia. Fur trim, embroidery and plaited borders were used to decorate clothes that were dyed in a range of colours, including blue, red and brown. Women normally wore long woollen dresses that reached down to their feet and were held in place by shoulder straps and brooches. The dresses were worn over an inner dress, or a type of long petticoat, usually made from a softer material such as linen. As Ibn Fadlan describes, most women wore a chain with a

Above left: The remains of a tapestry discovered in the Oseberg Ship burial. Parts of the tapestry give rare depictions of Viking women.

Above right: Strips of Persian silk found aboard the Oseberg Ship. Silk was a rare luxury from the east: most Viking clothes were made from wool and linen.

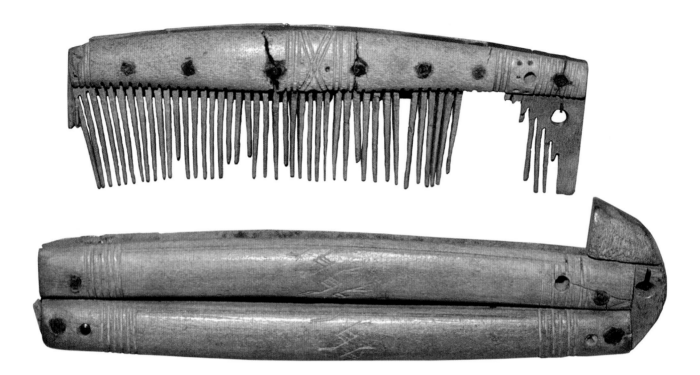

Above: A bone and deer-antler comb excavated from the Viking settlement at York, England.

useful implement hanging from it, such as a knife. Later in the Viking Age a shawl became a fashionable item to wear over a dress.

Men's clothes, made from the same materials as women's, included long tunics over a softer undershirt, with a heavy cloak fastened with a brooch at the shoulder, leaving the sword arm free. Viking trousers ranged from knee- to ankle-length, sometimes worn with stockings. Linen armbands were wrapped around the wrists and a cap or headband finished off the ensemble. While no complete Viking outfit has even been discovered, there are plenty of examples of footwear. These were leather shoes and boots, crafted by a cobbler and fastened to the foot with straps.

There are contradictory accounts about the care Vikings paid to their appearance. Ibn Fadlan refers to the Rus as "the filthiest of all Allah's creatures –

they do not clean themselves after excreting or urinating or wash themselves when in a state of ritual impurity [after coitus] and do not wash their hands after food." However, Fadlan's assessment is in contrast to that of English monk John of Wallingford, who writes that the Vikings' careful grooming won them great success with the women of England:

"They had also conquered, or planned to conquer, all the country's best cities and caused many hardships for the country's original citizens, for they were – according to their country's customs – in the habit of combing their hair every day, to bathe every Saturday, to change their clothes frequently and to draw attention to themselves by means of many such frivolous whims. In this way, they besieged the married women's virtue and

persuaded the daughters of even noble men to become their mistresses."
– John Wallingford, *The Chronicle of John of Wallingford*, translated by William Hunt

The idea that Viking men were interested in the way they looked is strengthened by the carvings on the wooden wagon from the Oseberg Ship burial. These show well-groomed warriors with combed hair and neatly plaited moustaches and beards. Fashionable Viking men seemed to have worn their hair long, with a fringe at the front and short, or shaved, at the back. Beards were worn long or short, but were kept neatly clipped and the hair shaved at the lower neck. Archeological items from both Scandinavia and settlements abroad also seem to confirm the Viking warrior's bent for preening: combs, tweezers, nail cleaners and washbowls have all been discovered in warrior graves. It was also considered a direct insult to a Viking's honour if another man intentionally made him dirty or tore his clothing. The punishment for these "crimes" was outlawry.

Other eyewitness accounts indicate that Viking men were not only vain, but also leaders of fashion. The Spanish Arab writer Al-Tartushi, visiting Denmark's Hedeby in the tenth century, noted that both men and women wore eye-makeup; and in an anonymous Old English letter, a man warns his brother not to give in to "Danish fashion with a shaved neck and blinded eyes" (blinded eyes probably means

a fringe in this instance). An English drawing of the Danish king of England, Cnut, shows him elegantly dressed with neat shoes and stockings, a knee-length tunic and cloak, both ornamented with decorative trimming. The fourteenth-century manuscript *Flateyjarbók* shows Harald Finehair, king of Norway, in a similar style to Cnut, with carefully combed hair and a belted tunic.

While these images perhaps contradict the common view of rough, unkempt and unclean Viking warriors, it is worth considering that they are all

made by Viking craftsmen from the most desirable materials of the time – silver and gold. The most common piece of jewellery was the brooch, worn by all women.

Most Viking jewellery was functional as well as decorative: brooches fastened a woman's dress at her shoulder and kept shawls and cloaks in place. All Viking females, rich and poor alike, owned at least two. Often oval in shape and featuring an animal design, brooches were cast from gold or silver for wealthy patrons or mass-produced base-metal imitations for the less wealthy. One silver brooch found at a burial site

> *"They were – according to their country's customs – in the habit of combing their hair every day, to bathe every Saturday, to change their clothes frequently."*
>
> — *John Wallingford*

associated with the wealthier members of Scandinavian society. Virtually nothing is known about the clothes worn by thralls and the poor, but it can be assumed these were of a very basic standard made from simple materials with little adherence to fashion.

Jewellery
Viking jewellery was lavish, ornate and intricately styled to show off the wearer's wealth and social position. Bespoke jewellery was

weighed around 1kg (2.2lb) and must have been worn with a heavy fur cloak for ceremonial occasions.

Other common pieces of jewellery were finger rings, neck rings, necklaces, pins and pendants, sometimes featuring pagan symbols such as Thor's hammer Mjöllnir and, later, crucifixes. Necklaces were ornamented with coloured beads such as cornelians and crystals from abroad or locally-sourced amber and glass. Neck and arm

rings were often fashioned from rods of gold or silver twisted together, while smaller versions were made for the fingers. Many of the rings found in Scandinavia were made from silver melted down from the thin Arabic coins called "dirhams". Silver was much sought-after during the Viking Age and the currency most commonly used for trading. Slaves were exchanged for the agreed weight in silver dirhams.

The wearing of many silver rings was a statement about a Viking's wealth, or, for a woman, about the status of her husband. The Arab diplomat Ibn Fadlan describes the wearing of jewellery for exactly this purpose among the Rus:

"The women wear neck rings of gold and silver, one for each 10,000 dirhams that her husband is worth; some women have many. Their most prized ornaments are beads of green glass of the same make as ceramic objects one finds on their ships. They trade beads among themselves and they pay an exaggerated price for them, for they buy them for a dirham apiece. They string them as necklaces for their women."

– Ibn Fadlan, *Risala*, translated by H.M. Smyser

Wearing silver jewellery was also a convenient way of carrying around one's fortune. A piece could be cut off as required or the whole item simply traded. The thirteenth century Icelandic author Snorri Sturluson reports that a skald was awarded a silver brooch weighing nearly 11.33kg (25lb) for a particularly moving nationalistic poem. The poet then cut the brooch into pieces and bought himself a farm. The purpose behind wearing silver jewellery was therefore twofold, especially for trading Vikings: it gave them immediate access to their own wealth, while also providing the wearer with the required prestige.

Women

Viking Age Scandinavia was a world dominated by men, but women were far from being underlings. Instead, Viking women were respected and independent members of society who were expected to participate equally in family decisions, run all matters pertaining to the household and be the leading figure of authority

while their husbands were away. Women were not permitted to carry weapons, but violence against Viking women was taken very seriously. A man who treated his wife violently would be hunted down by a group of Vikings banding together in the manner of a cowboy posse seeking retribution.

Despite their relatively similar social status to men, Viking women had clearly defined traditional roles. Men were responsible for farming, hunting, fishing, trading and fighting; a woman's duties centred around the home. They ground grain for bread, spun and wove wool, looked after the children, managed the

Above: This bronze brooch features two goats on either side of a "Thunderstone" representing Thor. The two male goats, Tandgnjost and Tandgrisner, drew Thor's chariot and were associated with masculine virility and creative energy. The brooch was part of hoard discovered in a grave in Birka dating from 983.

Left: A tenth century silver bracelet excavated from a Viking settlement in Ireland.

Facing page: A Norwegian filigree brooch fashioned in the so-called "Jellinge style".

Above: A re-enactor attempts to recreate the daily life of a Viking woman.

thralls and prepared the meals. However, family honour was as important to the women as to the men. Viking wives had a reputation for being proud and strong – they would encourage vengeance for wrongs committed against the family and erect runestones to their menfolk killed in battle. There is no evidence to suggest that women fought alongside their husbands in times of war but they did follow them abroad, including during foreign campaigns.

Marriages were usually an arranged alliance between families. The family of the wife-to-be provided a dowry and the prospective husband a similar sum – both of these payments went to the wife after the wedding. Married women had similar rights to men, including the legal right to divorce their husbands. The law also protected women from sexual harassment, including unwanted kissing and intercourse. Adultery, on the other hand, was severely punished – guilty husbands could be given the death penalty and guilty wives sold into slavery. However, husbands were legally allowed to have sex with as many concubines and female thralls as they liked. Sometimes, powerful Viking warriors were paired with concubines from families wishing to advance socially, although concubines had no legal rights and were of little threat to the Viking's wife in this sense. Children born of a concubinal union similarly had no legal standing or claim to their father's estate.

Little is known about children during the Viking Age and only a few graves containing child remains have been found. Some of these have included toys, such as models of ships and animals. It is known that unwanted or "abnormal" babies were killed by being exposed to the elements. Those who survived their childhood were expected to grow up fast and participate in many of the household chores.

LONGHOUSE LIFE AND THE LAW

The Viking's home was the longhouse, a building in a fenced-off homestead alongside several outhouses that served as weaving rooms, storehouses, workshops and smithies. Normally the farm animals shared the longhouse in a gable room at the end. Longhouses

Below: A woman and child re-enact life in a Viking trading camp. There is very little information about the lives of children in the Viking world.

Longhouse Hygiene

Domesticated animals were often allowed to share Viking longhouses, especially in the northerly Arctic regions of Norway and Sweden where they would have otherwise perished in the freezing conditions outside. However, a recent study of a 1000-year old Viking latrine by the University of Copenhagen showed that the close proximity of the people with their animals and their cesspits outside made conditions in Viking longhouses extremely unsanitary. Viking faeces contained many parasitical eggs from roundworm, human whipworm and liver fluke. Viking faeces found in Dublin were similarly infested. There was no known treatment for intestinal worms during the Viking Age, and their presence would have shortened people's lives as well as making them unthinkably uncomfortable. Although members of the Viking aristocracy used washbowls before a meal, the lack of running water combined with the generally poor levels of hygiene and sanitation around a Viking longhouse made perfect conditions for the spread of harmful germs. Vikings abroad certainly did not seem overly concerned with hygienic morning ablutions, as the Arab diplomat Ibn Fadlan reports of the Rus in the east:

"Every morning a girl comes and brings a tub of water and places it before her master. In this he proceeds to wash his face and hands and then his hair, combing it out over the vessel. Thereupon he blows his nose, and spits into the tub, and, leaving no dirt behind, conveys it all into this water. When he has finished, the girl carries the tub to the man next to him, who does the same. Thus she continues carrying the tub from one to another, till each of those who is in the house has blown his nose and spat into the tub, and washed his face and hair."

– Ibn Fadlan's Account of Scandinavian Merchants on the Volga in 922, translated by A.S. Cook

---

were built from the most readily available materials in the region. In the forested countries of Norway and Sweden, longhouses were made from wood with a layer of turf on the roof for extra insulation. In Denmark, timber was in shorter supply so longhouses were constructed from wood combined with wattle and topped with thatched roofs. In Iceland, where there was a scarcity of trees, longhouses were built almost exclusively from turf and stone.

The longhouses of the Viking nobility were large, lavish and opulently decorated with wooden carvings and iron fittings. The great hall at Gamla Uppsala is believed to have been a cavernous building around 200 square metres (2153 square feet), finely decorated and fitted with enormous wooden doors with an iron lock (stealing from any locked home in Viking Scandinavia was a crime punishable by death). It is believed the interior walls of the Gamla Uppsala great hall were regularly whitewashed, which would have given it a luxurious look compared with most dark and dingy longhouses.

However, even everyday longhouses shared the same layout and basic functions of the great hall at Gamla Uppsala. The floors were stamped earth, and raised platforms of earth and wood lined the walls. Inhabitants could relax on the platforms on layers of straw, furs and cushions away from the draughty floor. Other furniture included stools and chests, shelves for storing household utensils and tables for feasts. People normally slept on the raised platforms, but beds and the remains of a mattress stuffed with feathers have been found in the graves of wealthy Vikings.

Free Time

Viking leisure pursuits included board games and the telling of stories, but often long evenings would have been spent in more productive ways, such as carving, fixing tools or weapons, and weaving and sewing. After feeding the family, making clothes was the main occupation of Viking women. Even wealthy families who could afford silk bought in Constantinople and woollen cloth from Frisia spent many hours a

day spinning, weaving and sewing. Looms and the tools used for making cloth were often found alongside women in their graves. These typically include metal shears, bone needles and weaving boards.

An evening in a Viking longhouse would have been dark, cosy and smoky. The main source of light and heat was the central hearth, which lay at the heart of family longhouse life. The fire was kept constantly stoked for cooking and heating, but there was no chimney and it is thought many Vikings suffered from mild carbon monoxide poisoning in winter. Women would have been the worst affected, as they spent many hours next to the fire preparing meals for the family.

Meals and Food

There was much activity around the two main meals of the day, and women were buried with their kitchen utensils in the same way men were buried with their weapons. Even food has been found in Viking women's graves; the Oseberg Ship burial contained wheat, apples, hazelnuts, cumin, mustard and horseradish. Bread was a staple of the Viking diet and making it was time-consuming. Because the barley flour used in bread was ground on a quern-stone, small pieces of grit made their way into the baked loaf, helping to wear down Viking teeth. Bread was baked in iron pans by the fire and had to be eaten while it was hot or it became too hard to chew. Beef, veal, pork, goat, horse,

Above: A reconstructed stone Viking longhouse with a turf roof in the Shetland Islands.

"Better a house, though a hut it be,
A man is master at home;
A pair of goats and a patched-up roof
Are better far than begging."

— *Hávamál*

Above: A cutaway of a small longhouse, featuring the central hearth and the raised sleeping platforms around the outside walls.

Facing page: The interior of Eirik the Red's reconstructed longhouse in Greenland. Eirik's settlement of Brattahlid is today called Qassiarsuk.

mutton and lamb were part of the Viking diet alongside cabbage, garlic, peas and onions. Fish was consumed in large quantities and it was preserved along with meat for the winter months by being salted, wind dried and pickled in whey.

Small wooden washbasins found in the graves of wealthy Vikings were used before and after a meal. Forks were not known in Viking Age Scandinavia; people ate with knives and their fingers. Soups and stews were drunk straight from the bowl.

Beer, fruit wines and mead made

Facing page: A re-enactment of a Viking trading camp at an Icelandic Festival in Canada.

Below: Found on the Isle of Lewis, Scotland, these chess pieces were made in Scandinavia from walrus ivory and whales' teeth. Shown are the bishop, queen and king.

from honey were served at many of the feasts on long winter evenings. Beer was poured into horns, which encouraged consumption as the contents needed to be emptied in one long draught to avoid spillage and it was considered rude to put down a half-full horn. The sagas recall many stories concerning riotous parties, but, as the poem *Hávamál*, or "Words of the High One" reminds us, drunkenness was not considered a Viking virtue:

> "Less good than belief would have it
> Is mead for the sons of men:
> A man knows less the more he drinks,
> Becomes a befuddled fool."
> – *Poetic Edda*, translated by W.H. Auden & P.B. Taylor

Viking Feasts

Viking feasts were long bouts of self-indulgence often combining business and diplomacy. At the royal hall of a king or jarl, benches were set up and spread with cushions and coverings. Tapestries and cloth would be hung from the walls, and long tables laid out in front of the benches and set with fine tableware. The central hearth illuminated the room along with oil lamps and torches along the walls. Alcohol was drunk in large quantities, and fresh bread served alongside fish and meat dishes with cheese, vegetables, nuts and berries. Skalds and musicians with lyres, flutes and pipes provided the entertainment, along with the occasional juggler or acrobat. Viking feasts could

Above: Food fit for a Viking feast is displayed at the Lofotr Viking Museum, Norway.

Facing page: Shelves displaying the typical dishes and utensils used in the preparation of Viking meals, as exhibited at the Lofotr Viking Museum, Norway.

Viking feasts were long bouts of self-indulgence, often combining business and diplomacy.

last several days if the guest was a visiting dignitary. Author Adam of Bremen was present at just such an occasion, a diplomatic visit by the Archbishop of Hamburg-Bremen to the home of Danish King Svein Estridsson. Interestingly, on the agenda alongside the feasting was the question of converting the local population to Christianity:

"…as is the religious custom among the barbarians, they feasted each other sumptuously on eight successive days to confirm the treaty of alliance. Dispositions were made there of many ecclesiastical questions; decisions were reached about the peace for Christians and about the conversion of the pagans."

– Adam of Bremen,
History of Hamburg's Bishops,
translated by Francis J. Tschan

Above: Thingvellir in Iceland, the site of the Althing, which was held every summer for two weeks.

was to ensure that not even the king or jarl overseeing the Thing could try and alter any laws in his favour. Big decisions were made at a Thing – such as electing a new king, or the possible introduction of Christianity – and could last for many days. In Iceland, the whole nation gathered for the Althing, which was held every summer for two weeks at Thingvellir. The Althing was a great social event that included markets, feasting and the reunion of friends. Things were also held in other Viking colonies such as Orkney and Shetland and the Viking descendants on the Isle of Man still meet today on the mound known as Tynwald.

The king or jarl presiding over a Thing would mediate in disputes between two parties. Both sides were heard and the verdict voted on by those attending. Sometimes a harsh sentence such as death or being outlawed or sold as slave would be passed, but often a dispute would be resolved through financial compensation. The sentence of outlawry was almost as harsh as the death penalty – it meant the guilty man was banished from society, had his possessions confiscated and was allowed to be legally killed by any person who saw him.

The Thing

The most important decisions in Viking society were taken at meetings of the "Thing". Things were public assemblies of free men who would meet to discuss and vote on local political issues as well as legal disputes and matters of justice. A Thing was considered the highest court in the country, and it was opened by a recitation of the laws by "the law-reader man", who knew them by heart. This

Duels

In cases where financial compensation was not considered adequate, a duel could be ordered. Duels often followed an offence to someone's honour, which was of paramount importance to the Viking warrior and his family. The damage to honour could be material, such as burglary, physical

injury, destruction of property or dishonesty in business. More serious were verbal insults, such as calling a warrior a woman or accusing him of being sodomized. In these cases the warrior had the right to murder his defamer without sanction. Violent retaliation was not only considered the reasonable way to correct such wrongs, it was also encouraged. The law even allowed an aggrieved warrior to take his revenge against a family member of equal status instead of the guilty party. This in turn led to blood feuds between families that lasted for generations, as revenge killings followed counter-revenge killings until one family was wiped out or the matter finally forgotten.

An impromptu duel during a blood feud was called an "einvigi". This was an anything-goes fight to the death without rules or formalities. A more formal duel as

Above: An artist's view of the Althing. Big decisions were made at the Althing, but it was also a great social event where old friends were reunited.

Above: An anachronistic rendering of a holmgang, featuring the incorrectly styled horned helmets.

Facing page: The interior of a Viking fishing hut in the reconstructed trading town of Hedeby.

ordered by law was a "holmgang", with both parties sent to an island from which there was no escape. Unlike an einvigi, a holmgang had an elaborate set of regulations, which, among other things, dictated that the duel could be ended honourably after first blood was shed. Even more specific guidelines were sometimes given,

such as the exact area where the duel was to be fought.

In *The Saga of Cormac the Skald*, it was recorded that the holmgang between Cormac and Bersi was fought over an animal hide that was pegged to the ground by each of its four corners. The saga advises that a man preparing the animal hide for a holmgang should hammer in the pegs "in such a manner that he could see sky between his legs, holding the lobes of his ears and speaking the forewords used in the rite called "The Sacrifice of the Tjosnur". According to the saga, each of the combatants in a holmgang were given three shields, and if three were destroyed he would have to defend himself only with weapons. Then, if either man stepped outside of the animal hide or had his blood spilt on it, he would be the loser and have to pay "three marks of silver to be set free". This is what happened between Cormac and Bersi:

"So the hide was taken and spread under their feet. Thorgils held his brother's shield, and Thord Arndisarson that of Bersi. Bersi struck the first blow, and cleft Cormac's shield; Cormac struck at Bersi to the like peril. Each of them cut up and spoilt three shields of the other's. Then it was Cormac's turn. He struck at Bersi, who parried with Whitting [Bersi's sword]. Skofnung [Cormac's sword] cut the point off Whitting in front of the ridge. The sword-point flew upon Cormac's hand, and he was wounded in the thumb. The joint was cleft, and blood dropped upon the hide. Thereupon folk went between them and stayed the fight. Then said Cormac, 'This is a mean victory that Bersi has gained; it is only from my bad luck; and yet we must part.' He flung down his sword, and it met Bersi's target. A shard was broken out of Skofnung, and fire flew out of Thorveig's gift. Bersi asked the money for release, Cormac said it would be paid; and so they parted."
– *The Saga of Cormac the Skald*, translated by W.G. Collingwood and J. Stefansson

FROM FARMS TO FORTRESSES

Viking men lived in a violent world where attack could come at any time. They had to be ready to defend their honour against the slightest provocation, or protect themselves from blood feud and revenge. As raiders and invaders they spread violence abroad. However, at home the Vikings were also the main breadwinners and had to support their families through farming, fishing and hunting.

Farming was the main occupation of Vikings who lived on flat, fertile land. In spring, Vikings planning a summer of raiding or trading would first have to plough their fields and sow the crops ready to harvest on their return in autumn. Simple ploughs made from blades pulled behind animals cut through the soil, and iron sickles were used to reap the crops. Iron tools such as sickles and ploughs were crafted by a local smith, who also made everything from nails to swords. In single farm communities, the iron working had to be carried out at home; in larger settlements one ironsmith served several households. Travelling smiths also visited single farmsteads and more remote regions, and were specialists in forging weapons.

In Denmark, large settlements were typically made up of farming villages, although they often relocated every hundred years or so and permanent sites were only in place from late in the Viking Age. Vorbasse in Jutland is the only Viking village to have been completely excavated by modern

Above: A tenth-century CE silver arm ring discovered in Denmark. Arm rings were popular with both male and female Vikings.

Facing page: A cutaway artwork based on a Viking farmstead from the Danelaw in England.

archaeologists and it has provided a unique insight into a Viking farming settlement. Founded as early as 100 BCE, Vorbasse was moved several times within the same area until it became semi-permanent in the eighth century CE. The village did not move far – at most only around 75km (47 miles), probably to exploit more fertile land and leave behind the large deposits of human waste at the previous site.

The Vorbasse village was divided into seven farms, with a 10m- (33ft-) wide street running down the middle. The farms were laid out in similarly sized square plots, each with one longhouse,

several smaller buildings, a gate on to the main street and sometimes a well. Most buildings had sunken floors that kept them cool in summer and retained heat in winter. Each farm had between 20 and 100 cows, and dairy products, grain and iron tools produced in Vorbasse made their way along the trade networks to other parts of Scandinavia.

Towns

Scandinavian trading experienced a great upsurge in the eighth century and played a big part in the Vikings' expansion abroad. While long-range traders became rich from luxuries such as silk from the east, most early trade was short-range and took place within Scandinavia. Much of the local trade was carried out by part-timers – farmers turned merchants for the summer. But trading centres also attracted merchants as far afield as Spain,

the protection of a local king. He provided garrisons of warriors, extra fortifications when needed and, of course, charged a heavy royal levy on all profits.

Hedeby

There were two main trading towns in Viking Age Denmark: Ribe in the west and Hedeby in the east. Ribe provided the Danish gateway to northwestern Europe and it had solid trading connections with Britain, Frisia and the Frankish empire. However, Ribe reached its peak in the mid-800s and it declined as a trading centre soon after. This may be explained by the domination of Hedeby, which became the largest Scandinavian Viking Age town after King Godfred settled a colony of merchants and craftsmen there in 808. Hedeby sat at the base of the Jutland peninsula and therefore had control over the sea trade routes from western Europe to the Baltic countries. It was also close enough to the north German border that traders from Europe could travel overland to visit.

The main centre of Hedeby was laid out in a grid pattern with a stream running through its centre. It was protected on three sides by a rampart that stretched south to the Danevirke, a system of fortifications that separated Denmark from Germany. With the sea on its easterly side, Hedeby was divided into housing plots that backed on to the plank-covered street running through the town.

Hedeby artisans produced leather footwear, glass beads, pottery, bone combs and flutes, and silver and gold jewellery. It was also

Africa and Iraq. One of the first trading markets was Kaupang, situated in Norway's Vestfold by the mouth of the Olso Fjord. Kaupang means "marketplace", and its inhabitants did a roaring trade in animal furs, whetstones, iron, soapstone, jewellery, walrus-hide, rope and ivory. Goods unearthed from Kaupang graves show how cosmopolitan it was, with bronze items from Britain and glass from the Rhineland.

Kaupang was the main trading centre in Norway in the ninth and tenth century before closing in the eleventh century. However, it was not long before other similar Scandinavian trading emporia turned from small markets into bustling business centres. These thriving centres of commerce

became the first Viking towns.

The three most important of the Scandinavian trading towns were Ribe and Hedeby in Denmark and Birka in Sweden, all founded in the eighth century. The towns represented something new, modern and entirely unlike any settlement Scandinavia had seen before. They brought a brand of urban living in truly cosmopolitan environments, where local craftsmen and traders mixed with a multitude of different people speaking different languages and with different cultures and beliefs.

The new Viking trading towns became rich, overflowing with silver, gold and luxuries. They also inevitably became targets for pirates and raiders, and Ribe, Hedeby and Birka all fell under

a ship repair centre and the first Scandinavian coins were minted there. At the town's markets you could buy Frankish swords, basalt millstones from the Rhineland, Norwegian soapstone pots and luxury textiles from the east. Denmark's first church was also built in Hedeby by King Horik at the behest of the Hamburg-Bremen missionary Ansgar.

Although under the royal control of King Godfred and then his son, Horik, there is no evidence of a royal residence at Hedeby. However, a local ship burial known as the "boat-chamber grave" revealed items such as swords and riding equipment clearly belonging to a noble.

The reinforcement of the town's ramparts in the tenth century suggests it was expecting violent conflict. It was in fact besieged and invaded several times, notably by Norwegian king Harald Hardrada, who sacked the town in 1050. Hedeby fell into decline not long afterwards and the town gradually lost its inhabitants during the second half of the eleventh century. Nearby Schleswig quickly took over as Denmark's main trading port.

Hedeby did not impress all its foreign visitors. Here, Al-Tartushi, an Arab merchant from Spain, describes his experience of the town:

Above: The reconstructed trading town of Hedeby, Denmark.

Facing page: The Vikings were great takers of foreign coins and did not begin issuing their own in earnest until the late tenth century CE. These rare, early coins depict Viking longships.

Birka

Birka was a strongly fortified trading centre on the small island of Björkö in Lake Mälaren. Founded in around 800, it was Sweden's largest town. Its landward sides had a 1.82m- (6ft-) high earth-and-stone rampart topped with a palisade and tall wooden towers at each entry point. The main part of Birka was known as "the Black Earth" after its dark soil, and was overlooked by an oval-shaped hill fort. Between the sea and the houses was a flat strip of land to protect the town from an attack by fire. Many weapons have been found in Birka's graves and it is likely a garrison was stationed there. The grave of one high-status warrior buried in Birka included: two shields; an axe, sword, knife and dagger; 24 arrows; two spears; stirrups; two horses; a comb and a washbowl. The grave sites have also revealed more aristocratic objects: oriental textiles, Frisian jugs, Arabic dirhams and Saami jewellery. Birka's proximity to the centre of royal power in Sweden's Gamla Uppsala make it likely that nobles either lived in the town or close by. There is no question Birka was associated with royal power – it would have been built with a king's approval, protected by a royal charter, and it brought huge amounts of wealth into the court coffers.

Birka's 500–1000 permanent inhabitants sold furs, hides and iron from the north and lived in typical Viking longhouses, with smaller workshops for the manufacture of leather, iron goods and jewellery created from bone, beads, silver and gold. It is thought Birka had both a summer and winter market, and trappers and fur traders would have used skates and sleds to bring their wares over the ice in winter. Merchants from abroad would have arrived in summer when the sea voyage was at its least hazardous.

Birka's decline in 975 CE was sudden and mysterious. It may have been to do with the falling water levels in Lake Mälaren in the tenth century, but a more likely hypothesis points to the decline in Arab dirhams from the east. This was to do with the mines simply drying up, but it was also connected to the warring activities of the Rus prince Svyatoslav, whose conflicts along the Volga River clogged up one of the Vikings' main trading routes.

"Slesvig [Hedeby] is a very large town at the extreme end of the world ocean. The inhabitants worship Sirius, except for a minority of Christians who have a church of their own there. He who slaughters a sacrificial animal puts up poles at the door to his courtyard and impales the animal on them, be it a piece of cattle, a ram, billygoat or a pig so that his neighbours will be aware that he is making a sacrifice in honour of his god. The town is poor in goods and riches. People eat mainly fish, which exist in abundance. Babies are thrown into the sea for reasons of economy. The right to divorce belongs to the women. Artificial eye make-up is another peculiarity; when they wear it their beauty never disappears, indeed it is enhanced in both men and women. Further: never did I hear singing fouler than that of these people, it is a rumbling emanating from their throats, similar to that of a dog but even more bestial."

– Al-Tartushi, *Travel Book of Ibrahim ibn Jakub*, translated by H. Birkeland

Forts and Reinforced Frontiers

The tenth-century strengthening of towns such as Birka and Hedeby was part of a wider policy of fortifying the local settlements of Viking Scandinavia. At this time, the coastal towns of western Europe were fortifying their own defences against the Viking peril, and raiding became more difficult. The Vikings' own bustling trading centres became more vulnerable to attack. Sailing the waters around Scandinavia became dangerous for foreigners and Vikings alike. The Hamburg-Bremen missionary Ansgar encountered pirates on his way to the Swedish town of Birka. Here the journey is described by Ansgar's missionary companion, Rimbet:

"It may suffice for me to say that while they were in the midst of their journey they fell into the hands of pirates. The merchants with whom they were travelling defended themselves vigorously and for a time successfully, but eventually they were conquered and overcome by the pirates, who took from them their ships and all that they possessed, whilst they themselves barely escaped to land. With great difficulty they accomplished their long journey on foot, traversing also the intervening seas, where it was possible, by ship, and eventually arrived at the Swedish port called Birka."

– Rimet, *The Life of Ansgar*, translated by Charles H. Robinson

To further protect Birka and Hedeby from raiders, invaders and pirates, the seaward passage into their ports was booby-trapped with stone piles, wooden stakes and scuttled ships so only captains with local knowledge could navigate the harbours unharmed. Adam of Bremen, who visited Birka, reports on the tricky journey into a safe berth:

"Birka is the main Geatish town situated in the middle of Sweden not far from the temple called Uppsala … here forms an inlet of the Baltic or the Barbaric Sea a port facing

Below: The reconstructed town of Hedeby, which is today part of Schleswig-Holstein in Germany.

Above: A reconstructed Viking settlement near the town of Höfn, Iceland.

north which welcomes all the wild peoples all around this sea but which is risky for those who are careless or ignorant of such places … they have blocked this inlet of the troubled sea with hidden masses of rocks along more than 100 stadia [about 300m/984ft], making its passage perilous for themselves and for the pirates."

– Adam of Bremen, *History of Hamburg's Bishops*, translated by Francis J. Tschan

Fortifying the main port towns of Scandinavia was essential during

the violent and unpredictable Viking Age, but settlements in more rural locations were also vulnerable. Lookouts warned of attack by lighting hill beacons and people would find refuge in the local fortress. In Denmark, four such fortresses have been excavated: Aggersborg, Nonnebakken, Trelleborg and Fyrkat. Although built in different locations – two on the islands of Fyn and Sjælland and two on Jutland – they all follow the same design. All were circular, surrounded by a high rampart with a ditch beyond it.

Fortified Longhouses

One of the best excavated sites is Fyrkat, near the town of Hobro in northern Jutland. The fortress was built on a narrow ridge in a swampy valley, and many cartloads of soil were used to build the site up. The diameter of the rampart around Fyrkat was 120m (394ft), it measured 12m (39ft) at its widest point and was around 11m (36ft) high. Over 10,000 cubic metres (353,146 cubic feet) of earth and stone were used to build the rampart, which was faced with wood. A space called a "berm" between the rampart and the ditch was used to trap attackers and shoot them with arrows from the ramparts. The ditch itself was around 7 metres (23ft) wide and 2 metres (6ft 7in) deep.

Two streets covered with wooden planks ran from the

Below: A map of Viking hoards found across the Baltic states that contained foreign coins. Silver Arabic dirhams made up the mainstay of the Viking currency until 965 CE, when the supply dried up. From then on, the Vikings turned to England for their coins.

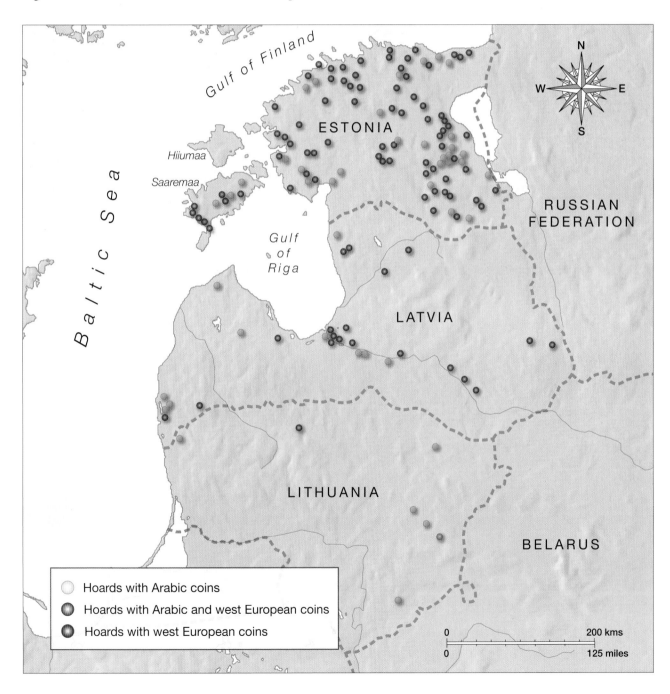

Hoards with Arabic coins

Hoards with Arabic and west European coins

Hoards with west European coins

Below: A reconstructed longhouse at Fyrkat, Denmark. Fyrkat was one of four ring fortresses constructed by Harald Bluetooth or his son Svein Forkbeard.

four entrances and crossed in the fortress centre. There were 16 buildings, some of them probably dwellings as they contained hearths, and others that may have been workshops, smithies, storerooms and barns. Outside the Fyrkat's ramparts was a cemetery. There is not an abundance of weapons to suggest the fortress was used only as a military barracks; neither are there any objects dating from beyond the eleventh century. There is, however, evidence of a fire, which was probably why Fyrkat was abandoned.

It seems Fyrkat, as well as Aggersborg, Nonnebakken and Trelleborg, may not have been attacked, but instead represent the rise of a centralized power in Denmark. The fortresses were probably built under the command of Harald Bluetooth or his son Svein Forkbeard, who wished to show off their military might to rivals both at home and abroad. Whatever their history of conflict, the fortresses represent the evolution of Scandinavia from a detached series of farming communities to a military kingdom governed by one central ruler, and thus its evolution into a nation state.

TRAVEL

Travel and the establishment of transport links were essential to the expansion of Viking Age Scandinavia, both at home and abroad. People travelled to markets, trade centres, Things and festivals within Scandinavia, while trade and war took people abroad. The many dramas associated with epic journeys made great subject matter for retelling as part of an evening's entertainment, especially if it was done by a Viking skald (poet). Trips across oceans made up the most exciting of these stories, but travel across land was just as important to the Vikings. During the Viking Age many causeways, roads and bridges were built to better facilitate these land journeys.

Most Viking Age land travel

Above: Viking ships were not only used for war: transport ships were vital for the carrying of goods and slaves between trading towns, such as the one shown here.

was undertaken on horseback or on foot. Vehicular traffic was also common and the wooden wagon found intact in the Oseberg Ship burial – albeit probably a ceremonial item only – shows the value placed on such an object for use in the afterlife. In winter, skis, skates, snowshoes and sleds were used for travel over frozen lakes and snowy ground. Fur trappers and hunters from places such as Norway's Hålogaland could travel for hundreds of miles like this, and did so to trade their wares at the southern market town of Kaupang. Viking skiing is also known from a runestone in Uppland and is mentioned in skaldic poems. One particularly memorable poem recounts the arduous journey of the skald Sigvat Thordarson, sent

The Danevirke

The most well-known fortification from Viking Age Scandinavia was the "Danevirke", a series of defensive earthworks stretching across the bottom of Jutland and cutting the peninsula off from its Saxon neighbours to the south. The Danevirke is thought to have been built as early as the sixth century CE, but it underwent major strengthening between 737 and 808 under the Danish King Godfred, who feared an invasion by the Franks. The Danevirke ramparts stretched for 30km (19 miles) between the trading town of Hedeby in the east to the Rheide and Treene rivers in the west. There were seven different sections of the Danevirke, each belonging to a different period and with a slightly different construction. At its strongest point the Danevirke was made of an earth and stone rampart 5m (16ft 5in) high, 20m (65ft 7in) wide and in places topped with a wooden palisade and fronted by a U-shaped ditch. The only way through was along a track known as the Army Road, which passed through a gateway in the wall near Hedeby. Despite the Danish Vikings' best efforts to stop an attack, King Harald Bluetooth's men were overcome by Saxon warriors in 974 and the Daniverke and border region around it occupied. In 983, the Danevirke was retaken by the Danes with the aid of warriors stationed at Denmark's royal circular fortresses.

Below: Part of the Danevirke fortification as it looks today. At its peak, the Danevirke stretched for 30km (19 miles) between Hedeby and the Rheide and Treene rivers.

"If you must journey to mountains and firths, Take food and fodder with you."

— *Hávamál*

on a diplomatic mission by the Norwegian King Olaf Haraldsson to Jarl Rognavlad of Västergötland, Sweden. The tortuous trek is retold in Snorri Sturluson's *Heimskringla*:

> "A hundred miles through
> Eid's old wood,
> And devil an alehouse, bad
> or good –
> A hundred miles, and tree
> and sky
> Were all that met the weary eye
> With many a grumble, many
> a groan.
> A hundred miles we trudged
> right on;
> And every king's man of us bore
> On each foot-sole a bleeding
> sore."

> – Snorri Sturluson,
> *Heimskringla*,
> translated by Samuel Laing

Thordarson also mentions travelling on a "crazy boat", where he became soaked to the bone. Travelling by sea, of course, was the Scandinavian tradition that gave the Vikings their name and made them the scourge of Europe. For the terrified coastal dwellers of Europe and beyond, there was no worse sight than the striped sails of a line of Viking longships on the horizon. To the monks of the British monasteries in the late eighth century, the Viking raiders were nothing less than apostles from hell.

Raiding

For over 200 years Viking raiders attacked the coastlines of Europe with such fury and brutality that some Christian monks believed they were being punished by God. As they prayed to be delivered from the savage Northmen, the Vikings plundered, slaughtered and enslaved local populations wherever they went. But the very first Viking raid was an entirely impromptu affair: a few ships, a handful of warriors, a bureaucratic official and a sudden burst of ultra-violence.

The first Viking raid on English soil took place at Portland, Dorset, in 789 CE. At that time, "a small fleet of Danes numbering three fast ships came unexpectedly to the coast; and this was their first coming", according to the *Anglo-Saxon Chronicle*. Hearing the ships had landed, a local official called Beaduheard leaped on his horse and galloped to the port. Beaduheard assumed the men were merchants and therefore needed to be registered in Dorchester according to the official rules.

Previous page - main image: Viking
raiders were the scourge of Europe:
they brought mayhem and destruction
wherever they went.

Previous page - inset: Early picture
stone of a Viking warrior.

However, something was either lost
in translation or the Vikings were
not impressed with this officious
administrator: they promptly
killed him and his retinue of men.
The Portland incident reflects the
common view of the Viking raids:
a few boatloads of bloodthirsty
warriors attacking unsuspecting
villages and slaying any who stood
in their way.

The first raids were certainly
small, uncoordinated affairs of up
to a dozen ships at a time, led by
opportunistic warriors chancing
their luck in the west. However,
this type of raiding was only the
curtain raiser. During the main
event, generations of Vikings
would raid with a murderous
intent. They cruised the coastline,
savaged seaside settlements
and then sailed up rivers to hit
vulnerable inland targets. Often,
the raiders would return to a

monastery, village or town that
had proved bountiful in the past
– those dwellings left standing
were often forced to close their
doors for good after multiple raids.
The attacks took place not only in
Britain – Ireland and Frankia were
both repeatedly struck, until the
incursions turned from raiding to
invading.

RAIDING LOGISTICS

In Britain, the early raids were
typically seasonal affairs carried
out by Vikings during the spring
and summer and who then
returned to Scandinavia to harvest
their crops. This initial phase of
Viking raiding, occurring during
the late eighth century and early
ninth century, was replaced by
a second phase of bigger, more
organized raids in the 830s. In
a third phase, beginning in the
860s, raiding was superseded by

invading and settling, as a whole "heathen army" travelled aboard large fleets with conquest in mind.

The size of the Viking fleets and numbers of warriors aboard them is the subject of debate. The *Anglo-Saxon Chronicle*, one of the main primary sources from the time, records one ninth century fleet of 35 ships. It does not specify how many men could fit on a ship, but an estimate using a conservative capacity of 50 men gives us a total of 1750 per fleet. However,

the *Anglo-Saxon Chronicle* also reports that a Viking force that attacked Paris in 885 CE was made up of 700 ships or 35,000 warriors using the above calculation, which is an impossibly large army for that time. We must assume the chroniclers often exaggerated the number of ships.

The number of Vikings found on a typical longship has had to be estimated by educated guesswork. The ninth-century Gokstad Ship had room for 32 oarsmen and

Above: A modern replica of the famous Gokstad Ship, which was probably owned by King Olaf Gudrødsson of the Yngling dynasty.

Facing page: An illustration of Norwegian Vikings raising their cups to a successful raid.

Above: *Skuldelev 5* was a 17.3 metre-(57ft-) long warship with room for 26 oarsmen. The longship's remains are housed in the Danish Viking Ship Museum.

Facing page: Some of the Viking jewellery and coins discovered at the trading town of Birka in Sweden.

hanging room for 64 shields on the ship's sides, suggesting 64 men were onboard who rowed in shifts. The later *Skuldelev 2* had 60 oars, but extra room for at least 20 more warriors onboard. The smaller *Skuldelev 5* only had room for 26 oarsmen. While it can probably be assumed the earlier raiding ships contained only warriors, captives and plunder, the later invasion ships also carried horses, wives and extra weaponry, which all took up a share of the available space. However, even using a cautious

estimate of 50 warriors per ship, a modest fleet of 20 ships could carry 1000 Viking warriors – a formidable force by any medieval standard.

If we cannot rely on the chronicles for exact numbers, they are accurate with the dates and locations of the Viking raids. However, what they fail to do is explain why the raids began and how they increased in size and frequency until they amounted to full-scale invasions.

So why did the raids happen?

Land in Scandinavia was scarce, especially in Norway. As the population increased, so did warfare, as regional Viking kings competed for the few resources available. As we have seen, Viking Scandinavia was a warrior society that believed in the necessity of warfare to ensure a place with Odin in the afterlife. Finding pastures new would not pacify the Vikings, at least to begin with, but it did direct their violence elsewhere.

The second factor was the rise of the trading networks across Scandinavia and beyond. The market towns of Kaupang, Birka and Hedeby introduced the Vikings at home not only to foreign people and cultures, but also to the quality and richness of their goods. Viking merchants were soon chasing these exotic products in trading emporia across northwestern Europe such as Dorestad in Frisia and Hamwic in southern England. These trading towns were always a target for pirates, and Dorestad and Hamwic

– along with Kaupang, Birka and Hedeby in Scandinavia – became heavily fortified and garrisoned as their wealth grew. But other settlements not far away from the prosperous markets remained unprotected and vulnerable: easy prey for pragmatic Vikings who would happily swap their trading hat for a raiding one. Monasteries – the main cultural centres of Medieval Europe – proved a temptation too far for many unscrupulous Vikings.

As we shall see, the inhabitants

Above: A dramatic nineteenth-century illustration of the attack on Lindisfarne.

of these monasteries viewed the raids on their most holy of places as a heinous crime against the faith. But, for the warriors who made them, the raids were a sensible form of enterprise – an entrepreneurial opportunity to make some capital that could then be sunk into trade, or a farm, or a ship. But it was more than that: it was also an adventure, an exciting rite of passage where warriors could sail the high seas, test their sword arms and win loot and glory. It was their chance to show their quality, forge a reputation and perhaps join Odin in Valhöll – these things and more were all

on offer for a warrior who went "a Viking" overseas.

Lindisfarne

England in 793 CE, the scene of the frenzied attack on the Lindisfarne monastery, was a green, prosperous and Christian country. After the Roman legions had deserted British shores in 410 CE to try and rescue their own lands from barbarians, pagan Saxons and Angles had taken England for their own. The country was broken up into four kingdoms that often warred with each other: Mercia, East Anglia, Wessex and Northumbria. Then, in the late sixth century, St Augustine introduced Christianity to England and the country entered a new phase in its history, centered around religion, learning and art. During this time, craftsmen created stunning jewellery and ornate metalworks in the new Christian Anglo-Saxon style; monks founded a series of monasteries along the windswept British coast; and pious scholars locked themselves away to write great chronicles with gold-embossed illustrations and gilded covers. One of these scholars was the Venerable Bede, who at the monastery at Jarrow in Northumbria wrote *The Ecclesiastical History of the English People*, completed sometime around 731. Then, 60 years later, as Britain continued to forge its post-Roman identity on a foundation of Anglo-Saxon Christianity, the peace was shattered:

> "793. Here came dire portents over the land of the Northumbrians, and miserably terrified the people; these were tremendous whirlwinds, and lightning-strokes; and fiery dragons were seen flying in the air. Upon these signs followed a great famine, and a little thereafter, in that same year, on January 8, pitifully did the ravages of heathen men devastate God's church in Lindisfarne Island, with plundering and manslaughter."
> – *Anglo-Saxon Chronicle*, translated by Rev. James Ingram

The monastery at Lindisfarne, an island off the Northumbrian coast in the northeast of England,

"...pitifully did the ravages of heathen men devastate God's church in Lindisfarne Island, with plundering and manslaughter."

— Anglo-Saxon Chronicle

was completely unprepared for the onslaught, despite the omens of doom described in the *Anglo-Saxon Chronicle*. On that day, the monks were in the windswept church when the Viking sails appeared on the horizon. We do not know if their longships were seen travelling to the shore at battle-speed, nor if they were heard being dragged up the sandy beaches. But we are given an account of what happened when the wild, bearded warriors from the north burst through the monastery doors with their weapons raised:

> "… and they laid all waste with dreadful havoc, trod with unhallowed feet the holy places, dug up the altars, and carried off all the treasures of the holy church. Some of the brethren they killed; some they carried off in chains; many they cast out, naked and loaded with insults; some they drowned in the sea."
> – Simeon of Durham, *A History of the Community of Durham*, translated by J. Stevenson

Apart from these contemporary descriptions gleaned from

eyewitness accounts but written after the event, there are few other details about Lindisfarne. Many men were killed, other taken as slaves and much loot was plundered. Amazingly, the *Lindisfarne Gospels*, a lavishly illustrated manuscript of the gospels of Matthew, Mark, Luke and John, was left untouched. Lindisfarne was a portentous moment. If the Viking raid had just been a repeat of Portland in 789 it would have left a mere ripple on the pool of English history. However, with Lindisfarne the warriors had butchered God's flock on consecrated ground – this was a shocking offence, an attack not just on the British church, but against Christendom across Europe.

News of the Lindisfarne raid soon reached Alcuin, a Northumbrian scholar living at the court of the Frankish king Charlemagne. He wrote a series of letters to England, including to Higbald, the bishop of Lindisfarne, and Æthelred, King of Northumbria. Alcuin was predictably aghast at the atrocities committed by the Vikings, but also used his letters to rail against the people of England:

Above: An illustration of the attack on Lindisfarne, showing some of the monks who were "carried off in chains" or "drowned in the sea".

Saint Cuthbert, with so great a company of saints, defends not his own? Either this is the beginning of a greater sorrow, or the sins of the people have brought this upon them."

– Letter of Alcuin, quoted in *Anglo-Saxon Literature* by John Earle

For Alcuin, the Viking raid symbolized more than pagan warriors pillaging a vulnerable coastal settlement – it was God's punishment for the sins of the people who lived there. "It has not happened by chance, but is the sign of some great guilt," Alcuin wrote to Higbald.

The shock and outrage of scholars like Alcuin over the violence of the Lindisfarne raid can still be felt in the modern age; the sudden horror of the raids is one reason the Vikings continue to fascinate us. However, while eighth-century Christians grieved and sought theological explanations for the murder of God's own, the Viking flood had begun. In 796, Northumbria was struck again, this time at the monastery at Jarrow where Bede himself had lived. In Scotland there was a raid on the Hebrides in 794. Attacks on Frankia and Ireland followed.

In 795, Viking longboats beached at the Scottish island of Iona and attacked its monastery. Founded in the sixth century by the Irish monk Columba, it was rich with donations left by Christian pilgrims. The raiders returned to Iona in 802 and 806, slaughtering dozens of monks with each visit. Those left alive decided to

"How have the heathen defiled the sanctuaries of God, and shed the blood of the saints round about the altar. They have laid waste the dwelling-place of our hope; they have trodden down the bodies of the saints in the temple of God like mire in the street. What can I say? I can only lament in my heart with you before the altar of Christ, and say: Spare, Lord, spare Thy people, and give not Thy heritage to the heathen, lest the pagans say, Where is the God of the Christians? What confidence is there for the churches of Britain if

abandon the monastery for a safer life in Ireland. But a few defiantly remained at Iona, determined to face the heathens and join the ranks of Christian martyrs. Their end was long and painful – the Vikings tortured the monks to find a supposed treasure hoard buried with the bones of St Columba. When torture failed to produce the desired information, those left alive were hacked to pieces.

RAIDING IN IRELAND

The Viking raids on Ireland started in the same way they did in Britain, as small hit-and-run affairs that usually targeted the country's rich monasteries. There were no towns in eighth-century Ireland, and monasteries were the economic and political centres of each

region. Local silver and gold was often stored at Irish monasteries, providing rich pickings for marauding pagans.

The *Annals of Ulster* records 26 attacks by Vikings in the first 25 years. However, Vikings were far from the only ones raising hell: in the same 25 year period the *Annals of Ulster* records 87 attacks from the Irish themselves. Ireland at that time was splintered into countless small kingdoms constantly at war with each other. Only the monastery at Armagh had any central power and control at that time, and the reach of its abbot, the head of the Irish church, stretched across the country. Other monasteries had authority only within their particular region, and were often

Above: Ruins of the priory of Lindisfarne, which was re-established in 1093 CE after the Viking threat had passed.

annis quod nos nostrique patres huius pulcher-
rime patrie incole fuimus. & nunqua
talis terror prius apparuit in bri-
tannia · uelut modo a pagana gente
perpessi sumus · nec eiusmodi nauigii fieri posse
putabatur · Ecce ecclesia sci cudberhti
sacerdotum dei sanguine aspersa omnibus
spoliata ornamentis locus cunctis in bri-
tannia uenerabilior · paganis gentibus
datur ad depredandu · Et ubi primu
post discessu sci pauli ni a beu boracia xpi
ana religio in nostra gente sumpsit initiu ·
ibi miserie et calamitatis coepit exordiu ·
Quis hoc non timet · quis hoc quasi capta
patriam non plangit · uinea electa uulpes
depredarunt · hereditas dni data est
populo non suo; Et ubi laus dni · ibi ludus
gentiu; festiuitas sca uersa est in luctu;
Atenti considerate frs · & diligentissime
pspicite · ne forte hoc inconsuetu et
inauditu malu aliqua inaudita mali
consuetudine promereretur; Non dico

"Never before has such terror appeared in Britain as we have now suffered from a pagan race."

— Alcuin

Above: One of Alcuin's outraged letters, which he wrote to Bishop Higbald and King Æthelred, among others.

the monastic communities of the northwest and southwest; by 830 they had circled the whole island. The *Annals of Ulster* records a raid in 821 on Howth in the north-east, where the Vikings "took a great prey of women" presumably as thralls or for ransom, followed by a savage attack on the island monasteries in Wexford harbour. The monks in remote coastal monasteries lived in perpetual fear, as a poem by one of them praising the bad weather indicates: "The wind is rough tonight, tossing the ocean's white hair; I fear no fierce Vikings, coursing the Irish sea."

From the 830s, the raids intensified as the Vikings began building "longphorts", or "ship-forts": fortified sea bases that allowed them to overwinter on Irish soil. Raiding was no longer restricted to the warm season, and the large number of slaves captured could be kept at the longphorts until the ransom was paid or they were shipped back to Scandinavia and beyond.

The Vikings eventually learned that there was a finite number of times one monastery could be raided, although many of them were hit several times. After a while monasteries simply could not replace the local inhabitants' gold and silver stored with the monks for safekeeping. The value of the ecclesiastical objects that could be quickly replaced – altar plates, ornamental mounts, crucifixes – was low. These were usually made of gilt-covered base metals, and although of interest to raiders as souvenirs, they did not hold much weight when melted down for resale. Instead, the Vikings found

forced to take sides against each other. The attacking and burning of monasteries, it therefore seems, was a national tradition far older than the Vikings.

The Vikings began their attacks on Ireland in 795. The early raids were swift, seaborne attacks on

The Lindisfarne Stone

The Lindisfarne Stone is a grave marker discovered in the ruins of the Norman priory on the island, and is thought to commemorate the Viking raid there. One side of the stone shows seven warriors dressed in jerkins, wielding swords and axes. Carved into the other side of the stone is a crucifix, the sun and the moon. Although the stone is thought to have been made in the ninth century, it has been carved in the style of Viking stone engravings usually only found in Scandinavia. The nationality of the gravestone and the reason for its creation remains a mystery.

Above: The Lindisfarne Stone is something of a contradiction: it is thought to commemorate the murdered monks, but is carved in the Viking style.

that more long-term wealth could be generated from the people taken from the Irish monasteries, both for ransom and for sale as slaves. Several large slave hauls from the late ninth century are recorded in the *Annals of Ulster*: 1000 people taken during a raid in 869 in Amargh; 280 captives taken in 886 in Kildare; 710 captured in another raid on Amargh, this time in 895.

If enslaving the local population of Ireland became a profitable trade within the Viking economy, there was no countrywide unification to stop this national outrage. The Irish survived the Viking raids and continued warring with each other. During the ninth century, however, the kings of Ireland began to fight back against the Vikings. Coastal monastery-settlements were fortified and, later, tall conical "round towers" were built as lookout points. Many Vikings left Ireland for raiding in Frankia or England in the later 840s after suffering a series of defeats by the

new Irish resistance. The Viking base at Dublin, controlled by Olaf the White and then his successor Ivar the Boneless, declined after Ivar died in 873. A period of peace called the "forty years' rest" followed. In 902, the Irish factions even came together for long enough to expel the Vikings from Dublin completely. But in 914 they were back. Within a few years they had established themselves in Dublin, Wexford, Waterford and Limerick.

By using longphorts as safe havens within these territories, the Vikings were free to carry out raids far from the coast. Longphorts were often based in existing monasteries, with the earliest known example built in 841 in Dublin. The Vikings knew that by building longphorts along rivers in the delicate border areas between two warring tribes they would often escape direct attack by the local inhabitants who wanted to avoid a diplomatic incident. Some longphorts were used for one winter only, and the Vikings stripped the surrounding farmland of food until they were ready to move on. The longphort in Dublin, however, became a permanent

Above: One of seven recorded Viking raids on the Clonmacnoise monastery in Ireland. The monastery was also attacked over 27 times by the Irish themselves.

Facing page: An illustration of the Viking raids on coastal Ireland, which began in 795. By 830, the raiders had circled the whole island.

The War of the Irish

An eleventh-century text about the Vikings in Ireland called *The War of the Irish Against the Foreigners* recounts the first raids on the country's coastlines. It describes the Vikings as "gentiles", "black pagans" (probably Danes) and "white pagans" (probably Norwegians), although it often confuses the two:

"The black pagans first came to the island of Britain from Denmark, and made great ravages in England; afterwards they entered Glamorgan, and there killed and burnt much; but, at last, the Cymiy [Scottish tribe] conquered them, driving them into the sea, and killing very many of them; from thence they went to Ireland and devastated Rechreyn and other places. They seem to have attacked at first the islands in which were Monasteries, possessing some wealth; and when they found that the spoils of these establishments were obtained with little or no resistance, they returned again in greater force, and attacked the mainland."

– *The War of the Irish Against the Foreigners*, translated by James Henthorn Todd

The text tells the story of the Viking leader Turgesius, "a Norwegian, who established himself as sovereign of the foreigners, and made Armagh the capital of his kingdom." Little is known about Turgesius except what is written in *The War of the Irish Against the Foreigners*, which at one point suggests he might have been the legendary Ragnar Lodbrok, which is doubtful. The work also describes Turgesius as something of a Viking superman "who assumed the sovereignty of the foreigners of Ireland", invaded the monastery at Armagh, made himself a pagan abbot there and attempted to convert the Christian population to the worship of Thor. Eventually, though, Turgesius met a sticky end: "Turgesius was made captive by Maelseachlainn, then King of Meath, and drowned in Loch Uair, now Loucrh Owel, near Mullingar, county of Westmeath."

Above: The Irish King Brian Boru is shown slain by the Vikings during the 1014 Battle of Clontarf.

settlement from 917. It grew into a fortified town and then a major trading centre.

This pattern was repeated not only in Ireland but also Britain and Frankia. As the towns developed, the nature of the Viking business changed, moving from raiding to trading. Viking warriors also became swords for hire, mercenaries employed by the Irish kings to help battle out

their differences. These constantly warring factions helped support the Viking economy in Ireland for several centuries, as children and wives joined their husbands and the raiding warriors became settlers. Dublin remained a Viking town until 1169 when Ireland was invaded by Normans. By that time, the Vikings had been mostly assimilated into the native Irish culture.

Above: An illustration of Magnus Barefoot, who became the last Norwegian king to fall in battle abroad after being ambushed in Ireland in 1103.

Above: Here, archaeologists excavate wooden footpaths in a Viking settlement in Dublin, Ireland.

Facing page: A fleet of Viking longships sail along the coast of the British Isles looking for raiding targets.

RAIDING IN ENGLAND

After Portland, Lindisfarne and the raids that followed in the early ninth century, Viking activity in England increased in 835. That was the year a Danish raiding party, fresh from sacking the prosperous Frisian trading centre of Dorestad, sailed across the English Channel and into the River Thames. Here, according to the *Anglo-Saxon Chronicle,* the "heathen men ravaged Sheppey", a small islet lying at the mouth of the river. Up until then, the raids had followed the same unplanned smash-and-grab approach used in Ireland during the same period. But Sheppey was nothing compared with what followed in 850.

Previously, Viking raiding had tapered off in the late autumn when the warriors sailed back to harvest their crops or overwintered in one of the emerging longphorts in Ireland. However, in 850 the *Anglo-Saxon Chronicle* records a Viking fleet of "350 ships" sacking Canterbury and London, and then setting up a camp on the Isle of Thanet to winter there. A second fleet appeared in 854 and overwintered on Sheppey. A third fleet then arrived and sacked Winchester, the capital of Wessex, before being chased away to Frankia. These Vikings were the new raiders, not content with slaves and silver from monasteries, but looking for a more permanent foothold.

Then, an entirely new menace emerged:

"865. And in this same year there came a great heathen host to England and took up winter quarters in East Anglia; and there they were supplied with horse;s, and the East Anglians made peace with them."
      – *Anglo-Saxon Chronicle*, translated by Rev. James Ingram

The size of this heathen army – a coalition of Viking warriors from the Scandinavian homeland countries – almost certainly measured in the thousands. More ominously for the Anglo-Saxons, these Vikings were no longer solely reliant on their longboats. Instead it was a landforce, one equipped with horses and wagons for long marches to inland targets. At the head of the army were two brothers, Halfdan of the Wide Embrace and Ivar the Boneless, who had been active in Dublin. Both were said to be the sons of the legendary Ragnar Lodbrok, whose raiding made him the scourge of England and France.

After overwintering in East Anglia, a kingdom that became accustomed to having its towns and villages pillaged, the "Great Heathen Army" made its way north to York, the capital of Northumbria. It rode through the gates on 1 November – All Saints' Day – when the city was packed with merrymakers and worshippers. Among those attending a service in York's cathedral were the two Northumbrian kings Osberht and Ælla, who had been too involved with their own civil war to seriously consider the pagan peril to the south. However, both managed to escape with their lives

Above: A Viking fleet approaches the Humber estuary in eastern England.

as the Vikings stormed the town.

After overwintering in the city, the Great Heathen Army left and Osberht and Ælla returned to take control. Once again, the Vikings returned to seize the city. Osberht was killed and Ælla captured. According to the Sagas, the brothers killed Ælla by carving the "blood eagle" on his back, a sacrifice to Odin that involved hacking out the ribs from around the spine and pulling out the lungs in a wing formation across the back. If the victim cried out during the procedure he was considered to have relinquished his right to join

Odin in Valhöll. The Great Heathen Army then installed a puppet king, initiated a string of attacks across Mercia, and travelled back to East Anglia to kill its king, Edmund:

"King Edmund, against whom Ivar advanced, stood inside his hall, and mindful of the Saviour, threw out his weapons… The impious one then bound Edmund and insulted him ignominiously, and beat him with rods, and afterwards led the devout king to a firm living tree, and tied him there with strong bonds, and beat him with whips. In between the whip lashes, Edmund called out with true belief in the Saviour Christ. Because of his belief, because he called to Christ to aid him, the heathens became furiously angry. They then shot spears at him, as if it was a game, until he was entirely covered with their missiles, like the bristles of a hedgehog (just like St Sebastian was). When Ivar the impious pirate saw that the noble king would not forsake Christ, but with resolute faith called after Him, he ordered Edmund beheaded, and the heathens did so. While Edmund called out to Christ, the heathen dragged the holy man to his death, and with one stroke struck off his head."

– Abbo of Fleury, *Passio Sancti Eadmundi*, translated by Francis Hervey

Ragnar Lodbrok

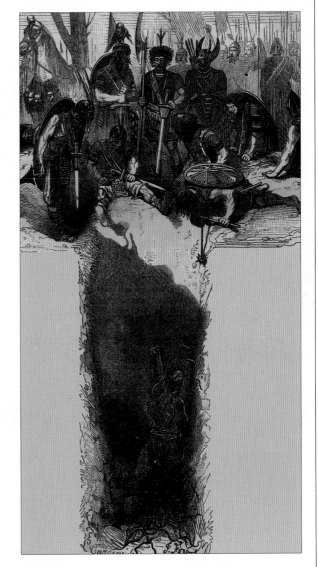

Ragnar Lodbrok, or Ragnar "Hairy Britches" as he was known, was one of the most notorious Viking raiders. Variously described as the King of Denmark and the warrior who sacked Paris in 845, Ragnar is often associated with the deeds of his sons, Halfdan of the Wide Embrace and Ivar the Boneless.

According to his eponymous saga, Ragnar became jealous of the fame won by his sons in England and decided to sail to Northumbria with an army. However, after a terrible defeat at the hands of the Northumbrian King Ælla, Ragnar was captured. Ragnar then irked Ælla by refusing to declare his true name, and as punishment he was thrown into a pit of snakes. This is where Ragnar's "hairy britches" came into their own. Said to be specially sewn of an extra thick fur, the snakes found Ragnar's trousers too tough to bite through. When Ælla saw the snakes were leaving Ragnar alone, the king had him hoisted from the pit, stripped and thrown back in. This did the trick: "at once snakes were hanging off him on all sides, and he left his life there with much courage." According to legend, Ragnar died with some fabled last words: "How the piglets would squeal if they knew the fate of the boar." It was certainly their father's fate that prompted Ragnar's sons to seek vengeance against Ælla – although his end was far more gruesome than death from a hundred snake bites.

Right: The legendary Ragnar Lodbrok is shown thrown into a snake pit, where he met his final end.

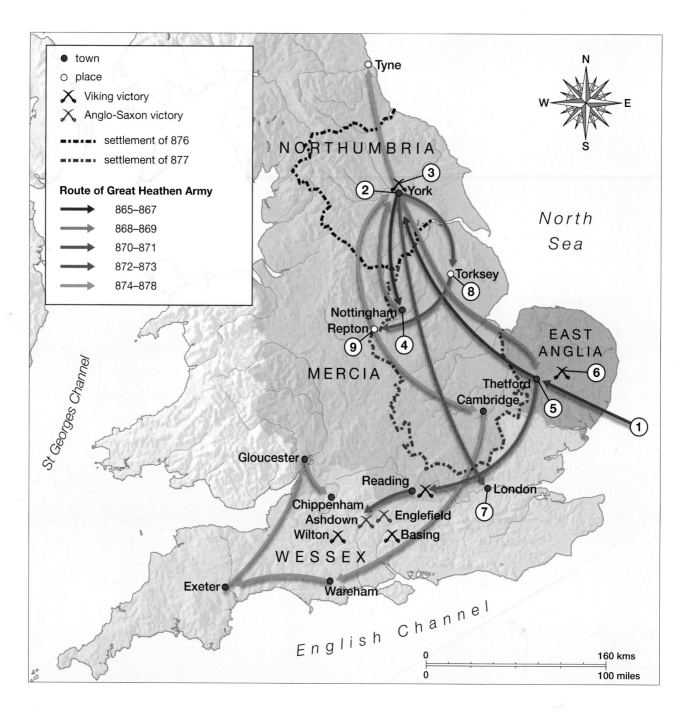

Above: This map shows the route taken by the
Great Heathen Army from 865 to 878.

1. 865: Great Heathen Army arrives in East Anglia.

2. 866: York occupied.

3. March 867: Danes attacked by the English.

4. 867–68: Danes overwinter in Nottingham.

5. 869–70: Danes overwinter in Thetford.

6. November 869: Edmund killed by Danes.

7. 871–72: Danes overwinter in London.

8. 872–73: Danes overwinter quarters.

9. 873: Great Heathen Army divides at Repton, sending
   armies to both Northumbria and Wessex.

Invading Wessex and Mercia

With Northumbria and East
Anglia under Viking control,
only the kingdoms of Mercia and
Wessex were left to be conquered.
But standing in the way of the
Great Heathen Army was King
Æthelred and his younger brother
Alfred. The legendary Alfred first
made a name for himself by taking
sole command of the Wessex army
at the 871 Battle of Ashdown. This

nearly ended in his death when
he rashly ordered a premature
charge of his warriors at the
Viking front line. But Alfred was
saved by the timely appearance of
Æthelred (late for battle because
his prayers overran, according to
legend) and his mounted reserves.
This was fortunate indeed for the
fate of England: Æthelred died
in the same year and Alfred was
crowned king of Wessex.

The *Anglo-Saxon Chronicle*
reports that thousands of Vikings
were killed at Ashdown and their
army put to flight, but after resting
in East Anglia the Vikings won
two major victories against the
armies of Wessex at the battles of
Basing and Meretun. The Viking
numbers had also been bolstered
by Guthrum, the leader of a new
"Great Summer Army", and now
he and Halfdan's Great Heathen

**Above: King Edmund, later to be known
as Edmund the Martyr, is ordered
lashed to a tree by Ivar the Boneless.**

Above: An illustration of Alfred the Great sealing victory against the Great Heathen Army at the 871 Battle of Ashdown.

Facing page: Alfred the Great disguises himself as a minstrel to glean information from the Viking invaders. Here, Alfred is brought to play before King Guthrum.

Army (Ivar had returned to Dublin to seek out opportunities there) combined against one of the two remaining English kingdoms still resisting them: Mercia.

The invasion of Mercia was swift and merciless, and in 874 the Vikings installed a puppet king at Repton, the Mercian seat of power. Now the Great Summer Army led by Guthrum prepared for a full assault on Alfred's Wessex. At first the invasion was something of an anti-climax. The Vikings attacked Wessex's border and then marched around its fortifications to set up a camp in Dorset. With his kingdom breached, Alfred hastily sought a peace treaty, but it was soon broken and more military manoeuvres and diplomatic initiatives followed. In the end Alfred paid the Vikings to go away, and Guthrum withdrew to overwinter in Mercia.

Guthrum, however, was not finished. He was still intent on conquering Wessex, and to dismember the state he would first have to cut off its head. Guthrum knew that Wessex's powerbase lay with its leader, Alfred. Alfred *was* Wessex: while he was alive men would still rally to him. So, during Christmas 878 Guthrum went straight for the kingdom's heart:

> "878. In this year in midwinter after twelfth night the enemy army came stealthily to Chippenham, and occupied the land of the West Saxons and settled there, and drove a great part of the people across the sea, and conquered most of the others; and the people submitted, except King Alfred."
> – *Anglo-Saxon Chronicle*, translated by Rev. James Ingram

With Alfred having escaped, Guthrum had missed his chance for an easy conquest. While Alfred was alive he was a threat, as the young king proved. Hiding in the marshes of Somerset, Alfred had no option but to conduct a type of guerilla warfare against Guthrum, now the oppressor of Wessex. Alfred would mount sudden, surprise attacks and then fall back into the shadows of the swamp. It was here that the legendary story of Alfred burning the cakes originates. The story describes a disguised Alfred taking refuge in a forest cottage. Here it was, brooding in his darkest hour over the fate of his kingdom, that Alfred burned the cakes that the mistress of the house had asked him to watch over. Alfred accepted

Above: Alfred the Great is scolded after famously burning the cakes.

Two-nation State

By cutting a deal with the defeated Guthrum, Alfred had forged the way for a two-nation state: one Anglo-Saxon and one Viking. In 886, the borders of these kingdoms were formalized. The Viking kingdom, or "Danelaw", would occupy the north of England; the territory roughly south of the Rivers Thames and Lea was Anglo-Saxon. Alfred immediately set about building "burghs", or fortified towns that his people could take refuge in during times of attack. Alfred's agreement with Guthrum was shrewd. However, it did nothing to address the rest of the Viking population outside the Danelaw and many new bands of raiders soon tried their luck on Alfred's shores.

The largest of these armies came aboard a fleet of 250 ships. It landed in Kent and confronted Alfred in a series of engagements before being chased into the Midlands and dispersing. Other Viking fleets were discouraged by Alfred's new navy, which saw off another Viking force in 893. To many marauding Vikings, England at this time must have simply seemed like too much trouble. Instead, they turned their attention across the English Channel to the land of the Franks.

RAIDING FRANKIA

The Franks, like Britain and Ireland, suffered for decades from Viking raids before facing full-scale army assaults on the heart of the Frankish kingdom. Charlemagne the Great had built coastal defences along Frisia, a realm that lay as a buffer

his sharp rebuke, and the episode represented the king's lowest moment and the turning point in his campaign against Guthrum.

In the spring of 878, Alfred was joined by men from Somerset, Hampshire and Wiltshire, who were fresh from sowing their crops and ready for battle. This new army, which was a force large enough to rival Guthrum's own, marched towards the Viking base at Chippenham, the place of Alfred's ousting during the midwinter. The two armies would face each other a few miles south of Chippenham, on a slope of land near Edington (see panel opposite).

The Battle of Edington

The best surviving account of the Battle of Edington comes from the Welsh monk Asser, who joined Alfred's court on the king's behest and wrote his biography in 893:

"Moving his standards thence the next morning, he [Alfred] came to a place called Edington, and with a close shield-wall fought fiercely against the whole army of the pagans; his attack was long and spirited, and finally by divine aid he triumphed and overthrew the pagans with a very great slaughter. He pursued them, killing them as they fled up to the stronghold, where he seized all that he found outside – men, horses and cattle – slaying the men at once; and before the gates of the pagan fortress he boldly encamped with his whole army. And when he had stayed there 14 days and the pagans had known the horrors of famine, cold, fear and at last of despair, they sought a peace by which the king was to take from them as many named hostages as he wished while he gave none to them – a kind of peace that they had never before concluded with any one. When the king heard their message he was moved to pity, and of his own accord received from them such designated hostages as he

Above: Alfred receives Guthrum at Aller after defeating the Vikings at the Battle of Edington.

wished. In addition to this, after the hostages were taken, the pagans took oath that they would most speedily leave his kingdom, and also Guthrum, their king, promised to accept Christianity and to receive baptism at the hands of King Alfred. For after three weeks Guthrum, king of the pagans, with 30 selected men of his army, came to King Alfred at a place called Aller near Athelney.

And Alfred received him as son by adoption, raising him from the sacred font of baptism; and his chrism-loosing on the eighth day was in the royal villa called Wedmore. After he was baptized he stayed with the king 12 nights, and to him and all the men with him the king generously gave many valuable gifts.

– *Asser's Life of King Alfred*, translated by W.H. Stevenson

between him and the Danish King Godfred. After Charlemagne invaded Frisia, Godfred feared that Denmark was next. He was right to feel this way: the plans were already in Charlemagne's mind. In response, Godfred built

up the border defences of the Daniverke and then in a show of bravado invaded Frisia in 810. Charlemagne had little choice but to pay 200 pounds (91kg) of Danegeld silver to make Godfred go home. It was the end of their

conflict; by 814 both leaders were dead and Charlemagne had been succeeded by Louis the Pious. But Godfred had paved the way for the next generation of Viking raiders.

While Louis the Pious battled for supremacy with his sons,

Lothar, Louis the German and Charles the Bald, the Vikings broke through the weakened Frankish defences. Their target was Dorestad, one of the largest trading centres in northwestern Europe and the jewel in the crown of Frisia. The Vikings sacked Dorestad in 834, 835, 836 and 837. One of the early Viking forays into the River Thames took place after the 835 sacking of Dorestad. The coastline of Ireland was also being mercilessly plundered at this time. In the heart of the Frankish kingdom, the floodgates had also been opened, and the terrible Viking tide could not be stopped.

Over the next few years the raids became regular and relentless: in 841 the Vikings sailed up the River Seine and sacked Rouen; in 842 the trading centre Quentovic was plundered; in 843, Nantes on the Loire was raided and the population slaughtered during a busy St John's Day; in the same year the first overwintering on the continent by a Viking force took place at Noirmoutier: here, the warriors set up camp "as if they meant to stay for ever".

Power struggles between Lothar, Louis and Charles, who had divided the Frankish kingdom following their father's

Above: The Vikings besiege Paris in 845. The Medieval city was then entirely contained on today's Île de la Cité.

Facing page: Charlemagne watches in dismay as a Viking army led by Godfred invades the newly annexed Frankish territory of Frisia.

Facing page: The Vikings used battering rams and flaming arrows to besiege the walls of Paris, but were repulsed with hot wax and pitch.

Below: A map showing the 885 siege of Paris by Sigfred, Sinric and Rollo, and the raids sanctioned by Charles the Fat which followed.

death, compounded Frankia's woes. Often the brothers joined with the Vikings to undermine each other's rule. Lothar, in particular, was known to have collaborated with the Dane Harald Klak during various raids, including on Dorestad, and the other two brothers also hired Viking mercenaries or nudged them towards their other brother's borders when it suited their purposes.

Viking raiding in Frankia became full-blown war in 845 when, as a Parisian monk recorded, "a vast army of Northmen breached the frontiers of the Christians." The frontier the monk described was Paris, victim of a 120-strong Viking fleet that sailed up the Seine and plundered the city. The invaders would not leave till Charles the Bald had paid

the Viking leader, Ragnar – later known as Ragnar Hairy Britches – a Danegeld of 7000 pounds (3175kg) of silver. From that point on the raids intensified and nowhere on Frankish soil could be considered a safe or sacred haven:

"The number of ships increases, the endless flood of Vikings never ceases to grow bigger. Everywhere Christ's people are the victims of massacre, burning and plunder. The Vikings over-run all that lies before them, and none can withstand them. They seize Bordeaux, Perigueux, Limoges, Angouleme, Toulouse; they make deserts of Angers, Tours and Orleans. Ships past counting voyage up the Seine, and throughout the entire region evil grows strong. Rouen

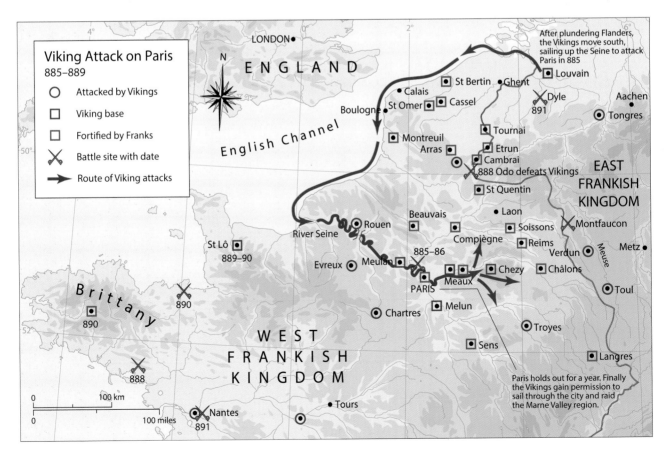

Above: Charles the Fat is shown agreeing the amount of silver to pay the Vikings to leave France: 700 pounds (317kg) in total.

is laid waste, looted and burnt: Paris, Beauvais, Meaux are taken, Melun's stronghold is razed to the ground, Chartres occupied, Evreux and Bayeux looted and every town invested."

– Ermentarius, *History of the Miracles and Translations of Saint Philibert*, translated by R. Poupardin

As monasteries, villages, towns and cities fell victim to the Vikings, all that the Frankish kings seemed able to do was to pay them to go away. Royal edicts were passed banning under penalty of death the sale of horses and weapons to the Vikings, but this did not stop the raiders growing rich from slaves, ransoms, loot and Danegelds. On one occasion Charles the Bald paid a large sum to a Viking army led by the warrior Weland to drive off another Viking army. But this army also paid Weland a share of their plunder, and the two armies wintered together on Frankish soil before sailing away.

Town fortifications and fortresses were hastily put up, but river mouths could not be protected and the Vikings often built their *longphorts* there. In desperation, Charles the Bald mobilized a large part of the male population to build fortified bridges, in the hope that they would block the Vikings' passage to riverside cities such as Paris. Charles did not live to see whether his bridges were effective; although they did not prevent the raids, they did play a part in the siege of Paris of 885.

The Siege of Paris

After Ragnar's humiliating plunder of the city in 845, Paris fell prey to the pagan warriors again in 857, this time to Ragnar's son Björn Ironside. Björn had left Paris in tatters; only four churches were left standing as he sailed away. After more attacks in the 860s, the Parisians developed a visceral hatred of the Vikings. This in part explains their determined efforts to hold off another band of raiders led by Sigfred and Sinric in 885.

Sigfred and Sinric sailed up the Seine at the head of a fleet of 300 ships to find the Île de la Cité – then the main centre of Paris – built up with towers, fortifications and two low-lying bridges. After being refused a Danegeld to leave by Charles the Bald's successor, Charles the Fat, the Vikings laid siege to the island. Despite attacking with battering rams and flaming arrows, the Vikings were repulsed. A two-month siege followed. The Vikings used various methods to try to reach the city walls, including filling in the Seine with debris and the dead bodies of prisoners, but to no avail. They even set three longboats on fire and sailed them towards the island, but they sank and caused no damage.

Below: The Tomb of Rollo, the Viking who became the ruler of Normandy and ancestor to William the Conqueror.

Vikings in the Mediterranean

Above: The ships of Björn Ironside and Hastein are shown landing in Italy.

The most famous Viking incursion into the Mediterranean was by Björn Ironside, who, after his wanton plunder and ruin of Paris, sailed down the Seine and out into the Atlantic to explore. Viking raiders had previously travelled as far as Spain. In 844 a reported fleet of 100 ships sailed around the Iberian peninsula, attacking Lisbon and then sailing to Seville, which they sacked and occupied for several days. However, after plundering the surrounding countryside, the Vikings were crushed by an army of Moors, who, according to their own accounts, destroyed 30 ships, killed 1000, and took 4000 Vikings prisoner.

Fifteen years later, Björn Ironside and Hastein, the Danish leaders sometimes said to be Ragnar Lodbrok's sons, followed a similar route to their earlier countrymen, sowing chaos along the Mediterranean coastline as they went. However, after a promising start, the 62-ship Viking fleet was ambushed by Moorish ships at the mouth of the Guadalquivir River. After quickly escaping the Vikings decided not to follow their predecessors to Seville but instead sailed through the Straits of Gibraltar to the Algeciras, which was ripe for the picking. The Vikings then raided the coast of North Africa and captured slaves there, before overwintering on the Balearic Islands and pressing on to Luna, the Italian city they mistakenly believed to be Rome. After sacking the city, the Vikings left a runic calling card. Today these runes, clumsily carved into one of the city's marble statue lions, are indecipherable – but their overall message is clear: "Björn Ironside and Hastein were here".

To get home to northern Europe, the Vikings had to survive a whole new series of skirmishes with the Moorish navy around the Straits of Gibraltar. The once-proud Viking fleet was badly damaged, and the survivors limped meekly for home. Only 20 of the original 62 ships would see the shores of Scandinavia again.

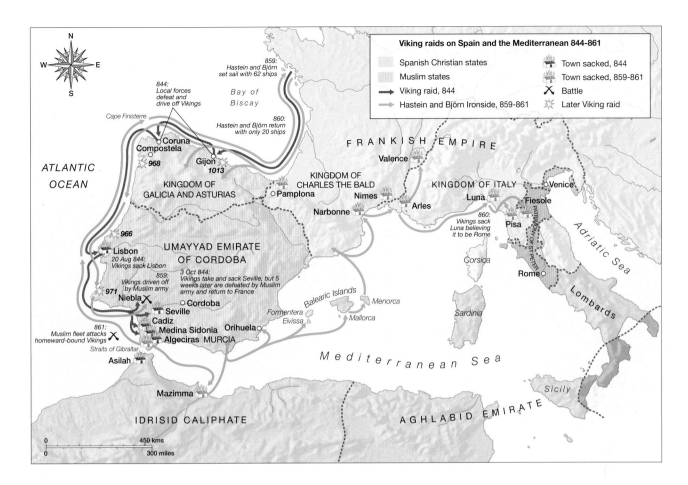

The following labels appear on the map:

Viking raids on Spain and the Mediterranean 844-861

- Spanish Christian states
- Muslim states
- Viking raid, 844
- Hastein and Björn Ironside, 859-861
- Town sacked, 844
- Town sacked, 859-861
- Battle
- Later Viking raid

859:
Hastein and Björn
set sail with 62 ships

844:
Local forces
defeat and
drive off Vikings

860:
Hastein and Björn return
with only 20 ships

Bay of Biscay

Cape Finisterre

ATLANTIC OCEAN

Coruna
Compostela
968
Gijon
1013

KINGDOM OF
GALICIA AND ASTURIAS

FRANKISH EMPIRE

Valence

Pamplona

KINGDOM OF
CHARLES THE BALD

Nimes
Narbonne
Arles

KINGDOM OF ITALY

Luna

Venice
Fiesole
Pisa

860:
Vikings sack
Luna believing
it to be Rome

Rome

Adriatic Sea

Lombards

966

Lisbon
20 Aug 844:
Vikings sack Lisbon

UMAYYAD EMIRATE
OF CORDOBA

859:
Vikings driven off
by Muslim army

971
Niebla

3 Oct 844:
Vikings take and sack Seville, but 5
weeks later are defeated by Muslim
army and return to France

Cordoba

Seville
Cadiz
Medina Sidonia
Algeciras

Orihuela
MURCIA

Balearic Islands

Menorca

Formentera
Eivissa
Mallorca

Corsica

Sardinia

861:
Muslim fleet attacks
homeward-bound Vikings

Straits of Gibraltar

Asilah

Mazimma

Mediterranean Sea

Sicily

IDRISID CALIPHATE

AGHLABID EMIRATE

0   450 kms
0   300 miles

After demanding 60 pounds (27kg) of silver and being refused, Sigfred quit the siege and was replaced by another Viking, Rollo. A final attempt on the city failed and in the summer Charles the Fat and his army set up a threatening camp on the nearby Monmartre hill. Charles did not really intend to fight: instead he encouraged the Vikings to sail away by directing them to Burgundy, which was in revolt against him and could be easily plundered. He then paid the Vikings a further 700 pounds (317kg) of silver to leave France altogether. Paris was saved.

Although the Viking leader Rollo had agreed to leave France, his time with the Franks was not yet finished. In 911 he was back and leading yet another siege of Paris. This time, however, the Frankish King Charles the Simple opted to make him an offer he couldn't refuse: land. If Rollo promised to convert to Christianity and protect the land later known as Normandy against other Vikings, it was his to rule over. Rollo accepted, married Charles' daughter Gisela and was baptized as Robert I. According to legend, Rollo refused to kiss the foot of Charles the Simple as a symbol of his loyalty and instead had one of his warriors to do it for him. However, this had the unfortunate effect of unbalancing the king and caused him to fall to the ground.

The Christianization of Rollo and the founding of Normandy symbolized the end of the Viking activity in the kingdom of the Franks. The last reported payment of a Danegeld to the

Above: A map showing the two Viking incursions to Spain and the Mediterranean. The second incursion was undertaken by Björn Ironside and Hastein, who led a fleet to the Mediterranean seeking plunder and adventure. Their final target was Luna, which they sacked, mistakenly thinking it was Rome.

Vikings was by King Rudolf in 926; after that the record books fall silent. The Viking raids ended on the continent, like those in Ireland and England, with the invaders going home for good, or becoming settlers and being assimilated into the local population. However, it is perhaps something of an irony that Rollo's descendants, including William the Conqueror, would bring the end of the Viking Age with the English invasion of 1066.

Warriors and Weapons

Viking warriors held a fabled reputation for their ferocity in battle. Christian chroniclers described their actions with horror, while the sagas praised their heroism. The warriors who stood out above the rest were men "…who rushed forwards without armour, were as mad as dogs or wolves, bit their shields and were strong as bears or wild bulls, and killed people at a blow, but neither fire nor iron told upon themselves. These were called Berserker".

The berserkers were the semi-mythological Viking warriors who foamed at the mouth and fought with a strength and frenzy that made their foes tremble with fear. It is the berserker that has given us the popular image of the Viking warriors. Some, however, dispute that they even existed. Still, stories about berserkers litter the Icelandic sagas, where they are both venerated as the most powerful of all Viking warriors, and also despised as ugly, unreasonable psychopaths.

The word "berserker" may stem from "bare of shirt", for going into battle without armour, or "bear-shirt" because of the animal skins that they wore. In the sagas, berserkers were also often associated with shape changing, and could take the form of a bear or wolf, or at the very least assume the qualities of these beasts before they went into combat. In *Haraldskvæði*, a skaldic poem about Harald Finehair, his

anyone who stepped in his way – friend, family or foe.

An incident where a berserker fails to recognize his family is told in *Egil's Saga*. In the story, Egil's father Skallagrim is taken by a berserkergang – called a "shape-strength" – as he played a ball game with his son and another boy, Thord:

> "Thord and Egil were set against Skallagrim in the game; and he became weary before them, so that they had the best of it. But in the evening after sunset it began to go worse with Egil and his partner. Skallagrim then became so strong and he caught up Thord and dashed him down so violently that every bone was broken and he died. Then he seized Egil. Now there was a handmaid of Skallagrim's named Thorgerdr Brak, who had nursed Egil when a child; she was a big woman, strong as a man, and of magic cunning. Said Brak: 'Dost thou turn thy shape-strength, Skallagrim, against thy son?' Whereat Skallagrim let Egil loose, but clutched at her. She broke away and took to her heels with Skallagrim after her. So went they to the utmost point of Digraness. Then she leapt out from the rock into the water. Skallagrim hurled after her a great stone, which struck her between the shoulders, and she never came up again."
>
> – *Egil's Saga*,
> translated by W.C. Green

Previous page - main image: A Viking re-enactment group forms a shield wall, the first line of defence used by armies across Europe during the Medieval period.

Previous page - inset image: A sixth-century bronze matrix depicting berserkers. Berserkers were associated with shape changing or the wearing of animal skins, such as the wolf costume shown here.

berserkers are called "wolf-skins" and in battle they "bear bloody shields and red with blood are their spears when they come to fight."

Berserkers are often recorded as being immune to injury or having "weapons glance off them". It is unclear if this is to do with the animal skins they may have worn or a greater tolerance to pain achieved by entering into a frenzied state. This state is often described as a fit of madness, a fury known as "berserkergang".

Berserkergang seized men with a chill that caused shivering, chattering of the teeth, a hot-headedness and a red swelling of the face. The berserkers then entered a great state of rage, where they howled like animals, bit the edges of their shields and attacked anything that moved. A berserkergang warrior was scared of nothing and would cut down

According to *Hrólf's Saga*, the great strength and immunity from pain

experienced by the berserker was immediately followed by a depleted state, where the warrior was "so powerless that they did not have half of their strength, and were as feeble as if they had just come out of bed from a sickness. This lasted for about a day." One way of killing a berserker, according to the sagas, was to wait until his fury had left and then attack him in the enfeebled state that followed. In the sagas, berserkergang was a condition that could seize men without warning. At other times it came over a warrior just before combat. There are many theories about how warriors harnessed the power of a berserkergang. Alcohol, hallucinogenic mushrooms or self-induced hysteria have all been suggested. It has also been

hypothesized that warriors underwent a ritual, which included a sacrifice to Odin and the drinking of wolf or bear blood.

It is known that Harald Finehair used berserkers as shock troops within his army, and other Viking kings employed them as personal bodyguards. It may be that these elite warriors were able to induce berserkergang at the required moment through ritualistic means. Reports of berserkers in battle variously describe them as fighting naked, or dyed in blue or covered in bear or wolf-fur – the latter was known as *ulfheðnar*, or "men clad in wolf skins". However valuable berserkers were within the theatre of conflict, outside of it they were often described as a blight on society. The Viking

Above: Great numbers of picture stones, such as this one from the ninth century, were found on the Swedish island of Gotland, where they often served as burial monuments.

Facing page: Bronze matrices, such as this one from Uppland, Sweden, were used to impress designs onto metal panels in the manufacture of helmets.

Hardbeen's Berserkergang

The berserker's place in society is aptly laid out by Saxo Grammaticus in his history of the Danes. Here, the berserker Hardbeen was known as both a fearless warrior and an untrustworthy sociopath who raped and killed at will. It is interesting to note in this account that Hardbeen's berserkergang comes on at the mere mention of combat:

"At this time one Hardbeen, who came from Helsingland, gloried in kidnapping and ravishing princesses, and used to kill any man who hindered him in his lusts. He preferred high matches to those that were lowly; and the more illustrious the victims he could violate, the more noble he thought himself. No man escaped unpunished who durst measure himself with Hardbeen in valour. He was so huge, that his stature reached the measure of nine ells [cubits]. He had 12 champions dwelling with him, whose business it was to rise up and to restrain his fury with the aid of bonds, whenever the rage came on him that foreboded of battle. These men asked Halfdan to attack Hardbeen and his champions man by man; and he not only promised to fight, but assured himself the victory with most confident words. When Hardbeen heard this, a demoniacal frenzy suddenly took him; he furiously bit and devoured the edges of his shield; he kept gulping down fiery coals; he snatched live embers in his mouth and let them pass down into his entrails; he rushed through the perils of crackling fires; and at last, when he had raved through every sort of madness, he turned his sword with raging hand against the hearts of six of his champions. It is doubtful whether this madness came from thirst for battle or natural ferocity. Then with the remaining band of his champions he attacked Halfdan, who crushed him with a hammer of wondrous size, so that he lost both victory and life; paying the penalty both to Halfdan, whom he had challenged, and to the kings whose offspring he had violently ravished."

– Saxo Grammaticus, *The Story of the Danes*, translated by Oliver Elton

Below: A silver coin depicting Erik Bloodaxe, king of Norway and York, and the last Viking ruler of the Danelaw.

warrior code demanded loyalty and fidelity to one's leader and comrades; berserkers, on the other hand, were known to turn indiscriminately on their friends and loved ones.

Outside of their role on the battlefield, the sagas often record berserkers as brutish murderers and sex offenders who lived outside the rules of Viking society. They are described as looking like trolls, with "black eyes and eyebrows joined up in the middle", and being "more like monsters than men." It is perhaps no wonder that as Viking Scandinavia converted to Christianity, berserkergang became unacceptable. In 1015, Erik Bloodaxe banned berserkers and made the practice of berserkergang punishable by outlawry. Later, the duels known as holmgang were also prohibited. This prevented berserkers challenging a warrior to a duel so he could take his property and women. The Icelandic *Egil's Saga* records such an incident:

"Gyda went to Egil and said: 'I will tell you, Egil, how things stand here with us. There is a man named Ljot the Pale. He is a Berserk and a duellist; he is hated. He came here and asked my daughter to wife; but we answered at once, refusing the match. Whereupon he challenged my son Fridgeir to wager of battle; and he has to go tomorrow to this combat on the island called Vors. Now I wished, Egil, that you should go to the combat with Fridgeir'

… On the morrow Fridgeir made ready to go, and many with him, Egil being one of the party. It was now good travelling weather.

They soon came to the island… Soon came thither Ljot and his party. Then he made him ready for the combat. He had shield and sword. Ljot was a man of vast size and strong. And as he came forward on the field to the ground of combat, a fit of Berserk fury seized him; he began to bellow hideously, and bit his shield… Ljot sprang swiftly to his feet. Egil bounded at him and dealt at once a blow at him. He pressed him so close that he was driven back, and the shield shifted from before him.

Then smote Egil at Ljot, and the blow came on him above the knee, taking off his leg. Ljot then fell and soon expired. Then Egil went to where Fridgeir and his party stood. He was heartily thanked for this work."

– *Egil's Saga*,
translated by W.C. Green

There are few recorded accounts of berserkers from the mid-eleventh century onwards. Like all pagan traditions such as spell casting and shape changing, berserkergang was considered a dangerous heathen practice that had no place in Christian society. Berserkers, alongside the god Odin they were dedicated to, disappeared from view.

Above: Two Rus Viking re-enactors fight a duel beside a longhouse. They are armed with typical Viking weapons – swords and shields.

THE WAY OF THE WARRIOR

It was not only the berserkers who belonged to a belief system governed by magic, the supernatural and gods of war. All of the Viking gods existed in one way or another to aid and protect their warriors. A Viking going into battle would do so with Odin, Thor and Freya looking over him; those who fell would be lifted to Valhöll by the Valkyries. The Valkyries were the terrifying demons of carnage that trawled the battlefield for the dead and had names like Shield-Scraper, Teeth-Grinder and Battle-Weaver. Old Norse poems also describe supernatural creatures such as dog-spirits and giant trolls prowling around the edges of Viking battles.

Objects associated with the rituals of violence were taken into combat – pendants, charms and amulets have been unearthed in warrior graves. One such find, a necklace of Thor's hammer Mjöllnir, belied the protective powers offered by the god: the warrior it lay with had been speared twice through the face, disembowelled and possibly castrated.

After the gods, a warrior's main allegiance was to his comrades in war and his jarl or king. Loyalty was bound up in the Viking honour code: following a leader to the death was a necessary point of honour; abandoning a leader in battle was one of the gravest crimes imaginable. This basic loyalty was shared by all members of a "lid", the name for a king's retinue of warriors. A Viking army was simply a large

lid that had come together for an offensive. Once the offensive or campaign had finished, the army would break up and the warriors travelled home or voyaged elsewhere to join another army. In the Scandinavian homelands, a levy system required all local men to bear arms and join their lord in an emergency.

A jarl was expected to lead from the front and spur his men on with an inspirational speech before battle began. A famous example is King Haakon the Good, half-brother of Erik Bloodaxe, who was immortalized in his death by his skald, Eyvindr Skaldaspillir. Eyvindr described the fateful morning before Haakon's battle

Above: The dying body of King Haakon the Good is carried by his men after being defeated in battle by the sons of Erik Bloodaxe.

Facing page: An artistic rendering of Odin, king of the gods, shown riding his eight-legged steed Sleipnir across the sky.

Above: A panel from the Stora Hammars I picture stone from Gotland, Sweden. The six panels depict war, human sacrifice and scenes from mythology.

against Erik Bloodaxe's sons. As Haakon rallied his warriors, he threw off his armour and joked with his men before charging into the fray:

"Haakon threw down his armour, thrust off his mailcoat
The great-hearted lord, before he took to the battle
Laughed with his men, his land he would defend now
The glad hero, clad in his gilded helmet.

The king's broadsword cut then keenly

Through foemen's armour, as if through water
Rattled then spear-shafts, war-shields were cleft
War-swords crashed onto the helmets of men.

Skulls and shields were trampled
By the hard hilt-blades and the gods of Northmen
Battle raged on the island, the king reddened
The shining shields with the shedding of blood.

Wound-fires burned in bloody gashes
Where the long-beards lifted against the lives of warriors
The sea-of-wounds surged high around the swords' edges
Ran the stream-of-arrows

to the Stord shore.

Reddened war-shields rang against each other,
Skogul's thunder blasts played against the darkened sky
Odin's storm billowed blood-red waves
As many a man's son was mowed down in battle.

Sat then the liege-lords with swords brandished
With shields shattered and shredded mailcoats
Not happy in their hearts was that host of men
As to Valhöll they winded their way."

– *Eyvindr skaldaspillir,*
Hákonarmál,
compiled from translations by Lee M. Hollander and Samuel Laing

The Royal Standard

The importance of the royal standard in battle was highlighted in an episode from *Egil's Saga* on the 937 Battle of Brunanburh. The battle was often considered the greatest English victory over the Vikings, second only to the 1066 Battle of Stamford Bridge, and was notable for its size and bloodshed:

"Then Thorolf became so furious that he cast his shield on his back, and, grasping his halberd with both hands, bounded forward dealing cut and thrust on either side. Men sprang away from him both ways, but he slew many. Thus he cleared the way forward to Earl Hring's standard, and then nothing could stop him. He slew the man who bore the earl's standard, and cut down the standard-pole. After that he lunged with his halberd at the earl's breast, driving it right through mail-coat and body, so that it came out at the shoulders; and he lifted him up on the halberd over his head, and planted the butt-end in the ground. There on the weapon the earl breathed out his life in sight of all, both friends and foes. Then Thorolf drew his sword and dealt blows on either side, his men also charging. Many Britons and Scots fell, but some turned and fled. But Earl Adils seeing his brother's fall, and the slaughter of many of his force, and the flight of some, while himself was in hard stress, turned to fly, and ran to the wood. Into the wood fled he and his company; and then all the force

Above: Thorolf is depicted running Earl Hring through and lifting him above his shoulders in the Battle of Brunanburh in 937.

that had followed the earl took to flight. Thorolf and Egil pursued the flying foe. Great was then the slaughter; the fugitives were scattered far and wide over the heath. Earl Adils had lowered his standard; so none could know his company from others. And soon the darkness of night began to close in. Thorolf and Egil returned to their camp; and just then king Athelstan came up with the main army, and they pitched their tents and made their arrangements. A little after came King Olaf with his army; they, too, encamped and made their arrangements where their men had before placed their tents. Then it was told King Olaf that both his earls Hring and Adils were fallen, and a multitude of his men likewise."

– *Egil's Saga*,
translated by W.C. Green

Above: A reconstruction of the Viking longhouse at the Trelleborg fortress, Denmark. There were 16 longhouses within the fortress walls, each measuring nearly 30 metres (98ft) long.

"A fair shield he had, and a helm, and was armed with a sword that was cunningly wrought."

— *Saga of the Ere-Dwellers*

Following a jarl or king's speech to his men, a Viking battle typically began with shouting, howling and the hurling of verbal abuse at the enemy lines. Chests would be thumped, quivers rattled and weapons clashed on shields.

Combat would begin with a volley of arrow fire and the throwing of spears. Then at closer quarters an army formed a shield wall – a battle formation of soldiers standing together with overlapping shields to create an impenetrable barrier. Two shield walls coming up against each other would spark a vicious shoving match, with warriors slashing at each other's exposed legs and heads. A contest between two shield walls could go on for hours, a type of battlefield stalemate that could only be broken when one wall tired and collapsed or tried to withdraw. A shield wall's strength lay in its unity, and when it fell apart it did so quickly and spectacularly. A typical battlefield melee would then follow as individual warriors fought hand-to-hand.

Warriors would look to their jarl for both inspiration and command on the battlefield. He would fight surrounded by a personal bodyguard and issue his commands via wind instruments. A Viking leader's men could easily pick him out in the chaos of battle by his standard, which was kept high by an especially strong and adept warrior. It was essential to keep a standard from falling in battle, and losing one was a catastrophe. One such example was a standard depicting a raven, the symbol of Odin, which was captured by Alfred's men during the 878 Viking defeat at the Battle of Edington.

Viking armies were highly mobile on land. They were used to marching long distances and then preparing improvised defences that suited the type of terrain or battle ahead. These defences could include palisades, pits and ditches lined with long stakes. Churches and other stone buildings were commandeered to form the centre of makeshift Viking forts, such as in Repton in Derbyshire. The Great

Heathen Army overwintered in Repton in 873 and made the town's St Wystan Church its headquarters. A "D"-shaped enclosure and ditch were constructed around the church, which gave a broad view of the surrounding countryside from its high steeple.

The aim of many Viking battles overseas was often twofold: first, to triumph over an opponent; and second, to exact a tribute often known as a Danegeld. When a battle was not won in definite terms, Viking armies were known to declare a truce by raising a shield up high. Terms of a peace treaty were then sworn on oath by the leaders of both sides over their weapons.

WEAPONS AND ARMOUR

A warrior's weapons were his prized possessions and they were buried with him for use in the afterlife. It was the right and duty of free men to bear arms, and carrying weapons was a

Above: A typical rendering of Viking warriors during a raid. Swords were a precious commodity among Vikings, and only the wealthiest warriors could afford one.

Far left: Viking swords, such as this one shown from the tenth century, were typically 60–90cm (24–36in) long, with a hilt and pommel to balance their double-edged blades.

Centre and above: The hilt of a sword was fitted with a crossguard, grip and pommel. The materials around these grips have eroded with time to expose the metal, called the "tang", underneath.

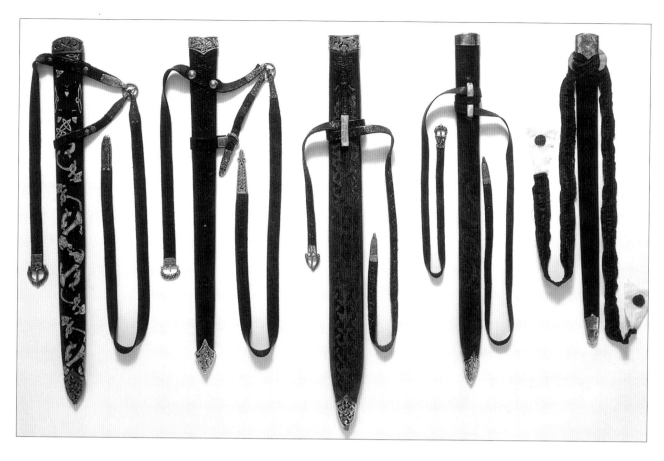

fundamental aspect of the warrior's being. Vikings believed their ultimate fate was preordained at birth, but everything else up until that moment was yet to be decided. Warriors were therefore encouraged to be bold in life, seize the day and forge great reputations.

Viking warriors fought mainly with swords, axes, spears, and bows and arrows, and protected themselves with shields, helmets and chainmail shirts. However, weapons were expensive and time-consuming to make. Only the wealthiest Vikings could equip themselves with the whole array of weapons, and the poorest warriors had to make do with a simple axe. The most costly weapon was the sword, and they were treated as precious family heirlooms handed down through the generations.

The great swords carried by

famous warriors were praised by the skalds and given names such as Leg Biter, Truce Breaker, Life Taker and War Flame. A sword was often a warrior's most valuable object, and losing one was a disaster. Weapons used in sacrifices to the gods have been found in a well-preserved state in bogs. It is these archeological finds that make up almost all of our knowledge of Viking weaponry.

Swords

A Viking sword was typically around 1kg (2.2lb) in weight and had a single-handed grip so a warrior could hold his shield in the other hand. The blade was tapered, double-edged and measured between 60 and 90cm (24–36in) long and 4 to 6cm (1.5–2.3in) wide. To give the blade its light weight it was given

Above: Scabbards were made from multiple layers of wood, leather and linen or fleece, and hung over the back or around the waist. Some scabbards came with "peace bands" to prevent the sword being drawn impetuously.

Right: One of the carved panels from Norway's Hylestad Church depicting scenes from the legend of Sigurd the Dragon Slayer. Here, Sigurd and Regin mend the sword Gam.

a "fuller", a central depression often decorated with inlays such as letters or symbols that the smith chiselled into the blade.

A Viking blade was forged using a process known as "pattern welding". This involved twisting and hammering together several red-hot iron bars. Soft, low-carbon iron was used in the centre of the sword for flexibility, and hard, high-carbon steel for a strong cutting edge. The blade was then fitted with a hilt – consisting of a pommel, grip and cross guard – and then polished to give it a mirror finish. Grips were often made from wrapped leather, but

Cutting Ties

Laxdæla Saga describes the importance of a sword to a Viking warrior. In the saga, Giermund is a rogue who plans to abandon his wife Thured and their daughter. But while he is asleep on his longship, Thured steals aboard to exact her revenge:

"She went across the gangway into the ship, where all men were asleep. She went to the hammock where Giermund slept. His sword Footbiter hung on a peg pole. Thured set their daughter in the hammock, and snatched off Footbiter and took it with her. Then she left the ship and rejoined her companions.

Now the daughter began to cry, and with that Giermund woke up and recognized the child, and thought he knew who must be at the bottom of this. He sprang up wanting to seize his sword, and missed it, as was to be expected, and then went to the deck, and saw that they were rowing away from the ship. Giermund called to his men, and bade them leap into the cockle-boat and row after them. They did so, but when they got a little way they found how the coal-blue sea poured into the boat, so they went back to the ship. Then Giermund called Thured

and bade her come back and give him his sword Footbiter, 'and take your daughter, and with her as much money as you like.' Thured answered, 'Would you rather then not have the sword back?' Giermund answered, 'I would give a great deal of money before I should care to let my sword go.' Thured answered, 'Then you shall never have it again, for you have in many ways behaved cowardly towards me, and here we shall part for good.'"

– *Laxdæla Saga*, translated by Muriel A.C. Press

Left and below: Viking battle axes featured wedge-shaped heads and "bearded axes" – a prominent bottom hook.

the remains of grips created from wood, wire, ivory and bone have also been discovered.

Despite the care and attention devoted to the making of a sword, not all swords were created equal. In *Olaf's Saga*, the king notices that his men's swords are not making the desired cuts, to which they explain: "The swords are blunt and full of notches." A smaller sword called a "sax", a single-edged blade of between 30 and 60cm (12–24in), was often crudely crafted and likely to fail. The sagas also record the blades of lesser swords as both bending and breaking in battle and having to be bent back into shape before combat could continue.

Similar trouble seems have been had with scabbards: the sagas recall bewitched swords sticking fast in their scabbards and scabbards falling to pieces so the sword falls out and is lost. A

Viking scabbard was made from wood, wrapped in leather, with an inner layer of fleece to protect the blade. The scabbard was often slung over the left shoulder or hung from the waist.

A sword without a scabbard was considered to be a problem, so much so that in *Harðar's Saga*, Inðridi refuses a sword in payment because it does not come with a scabbard. In *Olaf's Saga*, the king deals with Halfred, a skald he calls the "composer of difficulties' by presenting him with a problem to solve. He gives him a sword without a scabbard and commands him to compose a song about it using the word "sword" in every line. This is Halfred's poem:

"This sword of swords is
my reward.
For him who knows to wield
a sword,
And with his sword to serve
his lord,
Yet wants a sword, his lot
is hard.
I would I had my good
lord's leave
For this good sword a sheath
to choose:
I'm worth three swords
when men use,
But for the sword-sheath now
I grieve."
– *King Olaf's Saga*,
translated by Samuel Laing

The king then gives Halfred the scabbard, but observes that the word "sword" was absent from one of the lines. Halfred replies: "But instead there are three swords in one of the lines." "That is true," admits the king.

Axes

Axes are commonly associated with Vikings warriors and they made a cheaper and more available alternative to a sword. Even the poorest member of Viking society could afford to have an axe for chopping wood, which was a viable weapon if he was called on to fight.

Most war axes, however, were lighter, sharper and better balanced than their wood-splitting counterparts. Warrior axes were single-edged and made from iron with a hard steel cutting edge. An axe head was between 7 and 45cm (2.7–18in) long and usually featured a wedge shape. A "bearded axe" also had a wedge shape but also a prominent bottom hook, as if a crescent-shaped piece of the iron had been removed. The axe haft measured between 70 and 150cm (27–59in) in length, depending on whether the weapon was to be used with one or two hands. Even a two-handed axe could be light and weigh as little as 800g (28oz).

Although of less value than a sword, axes were often a warrior's valued possession and highly crafted with decorative inlays in gold and silver. Like swords, axes

Above: The great axes were given names such as "Battle Hag" and decorated with silver inlays, such as this famous example from Mammen, Denmark.

Right: Battle-axes were light and well balanced, and every Viking could afford to own one. As such, the axe was the most commonly used weapon on the Viking battlefield, alongside the spear.

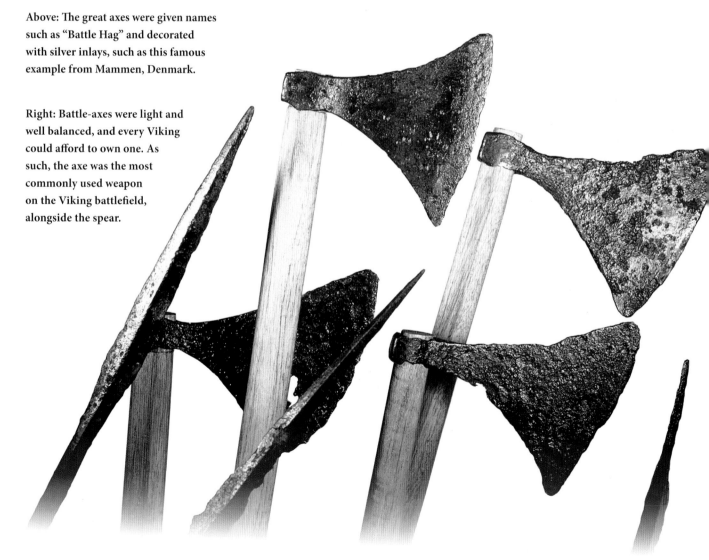

were given names, such as "Black Legs", "Heaven Scraper", "Drip Water" and "Battle Hag".

There are plenty of references in Viking literature to axes being used to split men's skulls, but their uses as a weapon ranged beyond just cutting and hacking. An axe's blade was also used to deadly effect, especially on bearded axes. They could hook away a defender's shield or weapon, or reach below a shield wall to pull an opponent over by his ankles. There are examples of warriors also using their axes to hook onto

a defensive wall or palisade and pull themselves up. The haft of an axe, sometimes protected with a leather or metal wrapping, could also be used to parry blows across its length or deliver a sharp jab from its butt end. Smaller axes were sometimes thrown, especially from the lines behind a shield wall, which also fired other missiles such as javelins, stones and arrows.

Despite the effectiveness of a Viking axe, the sagas record several occasions when axe heads shattered, often from hitting a rock after cutting through a foe's body

Below left: A Viking re-enactor holds a spear. Spears were used for both thrusting and throwing at opponents. The shape of spear blades ranged from spikes and leaf-shapes to those with barbs.

Below: Spears were not only cheap and utilitarian: this Swedish example boasts a finely decorated silver shaft.

part. At other times, axes could be the cause of accidents against comrades, as *Njal's Saga* describes:

"Thorgeir Craggeir runs thither where Thorkel Sigfus' son stood, and just then a man ran behind his back, but before he could do Thorgeir any hurt, Thorgeir lifted the axe, 'The Ogress of War' with both hands, and dashed the hammer of the axe with a back-blow into the head of him that stood behind him, so that his skull was

> ## "Gunnar strung his bow, took his arrows and threw them on the ground before him, shooting any that came within range."
>
> — *Njal's Saga*

shattered to small bits. 'Slain is this one' said Thorgeir; and down the man fell at once, and was dead. But when he dashed the axe forward, he smote Thorkel on the shoulder, and hewed it off, arm and all."

> – *Njal's Saga*,
> translated by George W. Dasent

Spears

Spears were arguably the most popular weapon of the Viking Age. A spear could be used by a wealthy warrior alongside a sword, or instead of an axe by a Viking of more modest means. Spearheads were typically between 20 and 70cm (8–27in) long, and once

riveted to a shaft the whole spear would be between 2 and 3m (6ft 6in–9ft 3in) long. The spearhead blade was made from the same pattern-welding technique as a sword. Iron bars were beaten into a lozenge shape that tapered into a hard cutting edge on either side of the spear and at its tip. Similar to Viking swords, spearheads were decorated with gold and silver ornamental inlays, usually of patterns or geometric symbols. The shape of the spearhead ranged from a long spike to a leaf shape and sometimes had wings or barbs attached, making them easy to penetrate and snag opponents, but hard to remove.

The sagas are full of examples of Vikings throwing their spears, although in practice this would have been done only as a last resort. A spear was often a warrior's sole weapon and he would not want to let it go. Instead of throwing, then, spears were most commonly used for thrusting and jabbing, especially at the vulnerable legs and heads exposed in an enemy's shield wall.

Using a spear two-handed gave a warrior the chance to hold it further along the shaft and increase his reach. The sagas also describe the effectiveness of the one-handed approach, giving the warrior a free hand for another weapon:

"Against Kari came Mord Sigfus' son, and Sigmund Sigfus' son, and Lambi Sigurd's son; the last ran behind Kari's back, and thrust at him with a spear; Kari caught sight of him, and leapt up as the blow fell, and

stretched his legs far apart, and so the blow spent itself on the ground, but Kari jumped down on the spear-shaft, and snapped it in sunder. He had a spear in one hand, and a sword in the other, but no shield. He thrust with the right hand at Sigmund Sigfus' son, and smote him on his breast, and the spear came out between his shoulders, and down he fell and was dead at once. With his left hand he made a cut at Mord, and smote him on the hip, and cut it asunder, and his backbone too; he fell flat on his face, and was dead at once."

– Njal's Saga,
translated by George W. Dasent

The length of the spear's shaft appeared to be its biggest drawback: spears were often reported as being snapped in two in the sagas; the spearheads themselves were similarly reported to have been hacked off. The Viking swordsman therefore was credited with having the greatest odds of success on the battlefield.

Bows

In Viking battles between two facing armies, archers began the hostilities before the two lines came together. Few remnants of Viking bows have been found, except one well preserved yew longbow at Hedeby in the Danish-

Above: Viking archers often opened fire from distance before two opposing lines attacked each other. They would then send volleys from behind a shield wall.

**Above: Re-enactors form a shield wall.
According to the sagas, warriors carried
red shields to signal hostile intentions.**

northern German borderland,
which has a length of 190cm
(75in). Generally, it is thought
the length of Viking bows ranged
from between 150 and 200cm
(59–79in). Many arrows have been
discovered in Viking graves, and
these typically had a length of
between 50 and 70cm (20–27in)
and were fitted with an iron tip.

The sagas recount many
episodes where Viking heroes
used their bows to slay enemy
warriors: in *Olaf's Saga* Gunnar
mowed down 10 foes with his bow
while defending his house; King
Olaf was reported to have fired
a multitude of arrows from his
flagship the *Long Serpent* before
his death during the naval Battle
of Svolder. The end of the battle
is then famously heralded by the
cracking of archer Einar's bow, the

result of a perfectly flighted arrow
from the opposite side.

Shields

Every Viking had at least one
large, round wooden shield for
protection in battle. Made from
wooden planks covered in leather
or linen, and sometimes painted
in bright stripes, shields would
accompany Vikings across the
seas and be attached to the side
of longships to give them their
menacing battle-ready appearance.
The straps that held a shield to the
ship was also used to sling it onto a
warrior's back for long marches or
to free both hands in battle. At the
centre of the shield was a domed
iron boss, which protected the
hand and could be used to punch
at an opponent. A handgrip on
the inside of the dome allowed the

Left and below: Vikings shields were generally round and often brightly decorated. The shields found aboard the Gokstad Ship were painted in black and yellow.

Below: Kite shields were the mainstay of many Medieval armies, but were not widely used by the Vikings. One exception was found in Norway, which dated from the late eleventh century CE. This one is decorated with a serpent motif.

shield to be rotated, and iron bars sometimes lined the back of the shield for added reinforcement.

Shields were between 70 and 100cm (27–39in) in diameter, and had a thickness of between 7 and 30mm (0.27–1.18in). They were almost certainly treated with an oil-based substance to protect against water, which in some cases was paint – black and white stripes were both used and skaldic poems describe shields being decorated with pictures of gods and heroes. The last line of a shield's protection was a rawhide edging, which helped to hold it together after it had been split in battle.

The splitting of shields seems to have been a common occurrence according to the sagas. In *Njal's Saga*, Thorgeir cleaves a shield in two with his axe, "The Ogress of War", and the blow continues into his assailant's collarbone and through his torso. For the Viking duel known as a holmgang, the rules allowed each man to bring three shields, suggesting at least one would be broken during the bout.

Shields were the obviously essential component of the shield wall, and each one was large enough to protect the area from the knees to the head. However, studies of the skeletal remains of Viking warriors show wounds to the legs and head were common. Also, being in the front line of a shield wall did also not bring much protection from enemy arrows. The sagas report several episodes where an arrow shaft penetrates a shield and kills the man holding it, such as this bout between Gunnar and Sigurd Swinehead in *Njal's Saga*:

"Gunnar sees him and shoots an arrow at him from his bow; he held the shield up aloft when he saw the arrow flying high, and the shaft passes through the shield and into his eye, and so came out at the nape of his neck, and that was the first man slain."
– *Njal's Saga*, translated by George W. Dasent

Chainmail

Like swords, chainmail armour was a highly desirable piece of equipment that only the wealthiest Viking warriors could afford. Viking chainmail was made of a series of interlocking iron rings with each ring looped through the four rings nearest to it. The chainmail was then fashioned into a shirt, usually with short sleeves and reaching to the thighs or even lower. In *Harald's Saga*, the king had a shirt called "Emma" that reached down below his knees.

A chainmail shirt weighed more than 10kg (22lb) and was made up of 20,000–30,000 iron rings, riveted in place for extra protection. The time-consuming task of making a chainmail shirt combined with the cost of the iron made it prohibitively expensive. Chainmail shirts were given as generous presents between kings; those who could not afford a whole shirt used strips of chainmail to protect vulnerable places such as the back of the neck.

The fabric of chainmail prevented a blade from penetrating the wearer's skin, but did not prevent bruising or broken bones caused by the force of the blow. To insulate the wearer from the

chainmail, an inner layer consisting of a leather and fleece jerkin was probably worn. However, the integrity of chainmail was also known to fail under a particularly powerful thrust from a blade. Such an instance is recorded in the *Laxdæla Saga*, when a conflict arises between Eldgrim and Hrut after a deal over a horse goes sour:

"Eldgrim now wanted to part, and gave the whip to his horse, and when Hrut saw that, he raised up his halberd and struck Eldgrim through the back between the shoulders so that the coat of mail was torn open and the halberd flew out through the chest, and Eldgrim fell dead off his horse, as was only natural."
– *Laxdæla Saga*, translated by Muriel A.C. Press

Above: Viking helmets were usually made from several metal plates hammered into a dome or oval shape. Only one complete Viking helmet has ever been discovered.

Facing page: Viking chainmail shirts were expensive and even the cost of the iron was beyond reach for many warriors. Few examples have survived into the modern age.

Above: Helmets often featured a nose and spectacle-shaped guard to protect the upper face. According to the sagas, these guards could be easily cut away.

Helmets

Although it has been popular to depict Viking warriors wearing horned helmets, this is a modern anachronism. Instead, Viking helmets were usually made from a simple bowl-shape with a nose guard riveted to the brow. Helmets were made from a single piece of hammered iron, or several smaller pieces riveted together and occasionally strengthened with strips of leather.

Some helmets were dome-shaped, or had an iron spectacle-shape to protect the top of the face. A chainmail curtain might hang down from the front of this spectacle-type of helmet or from the back to protect the neck. Some sort of cap or thick lining must have been worn inside the helmet to protect the wearer from the impact of a blow, although no archaeological evidence of these has survived.

Helmets weighed anywhere from 2kg (4.4lb) upwards and were kept in place with a chin strap. The sagas report that helmets were also marked, possibly with chalk, so that the wearer could be identified in battle as belonging to a particular side. Helmets feature often in the sagas as valued possessions passed down through the generations. They were also considered something of a challenge – an object that warriors liked to cast asunder during their skull-splitting activities.

LONGSHIPS

There is no more enduring symbol of the Viking Age than the longship. It was a masterpiece of ancient shipbuilding and enabled the Vikings' astonishing expansion around the world. It was also the most effective weapon in the Viking arsenal, designed to sail up rivers and to land on sandy beaches to conduct lightning-fast raids. Without the longship the Viking Age would never have happened and it was venerated in the culture of the time. The longship was honoured in burials for important leaders, it was immortalized in skaldic poetry,

Grettir and Snaekoll

No weapon could guarantee success on the battlefield. Here, Grettir uses the berserker Snaekoll's helmet against him in combat:

"The berserk was sitting on his horse wearing his helmet, the chin-piece of which was not fastened. He held before him a shield bound with iron and looked terribly threatening. He said to Einar [Grettir's host]: 'You had better choose quickly: either one thing or the other. What does that big fellow standing beside you say? Would he not like to play with me himself?'

'One of us is as good as the other,' said Grettir: 'Neither of us is very active.'

'All the more afraid will you be to fight with me if I get angry.'

'That will be seen when it is tried,' said Grettir.

The berserk thought they were trying to get off by talking. He began to howl and to bite the rim of his shield. He held the shield up to his mouth and scowled over its upper edge like a madman. Grettir stepped quickly across the ground, and when he got even with the berserk's horse he kicked the shield with his foot from below with such force that it struck his mouth, breaking the upper jaw, and the lower jaw fell down on to his chest. With the same movement he seized the Viking's helmet with his left hand and dragged him from his horse, while with his right hand he raised his axe and cut off the berserk's head. Snaekoll's followers, when they saw what had happened, fled, every man of them."

– *Grettir's Saga*, translated by G.H. Hight

Helmets were considered something of a challenge – an object that warriors liked to cast asunder during their skull-splitting activities.

modelled in jewellery and carved into runestones; it was the motif that best described the Vikings and their successes, aspirations and desire for adventure.

The Scandinavian tradition of boat building was thousands of years old by the time of the Vikings proper, although the earlier ships were smaller, narrower and powered only by oars. The sail was the most important development in the Viking Age; it enabled travel by day and night and it doubled the ship's power for surprise attacks at speed. However, the great warships used in the raids on coastal Europe were not the mainstay of the Scandinavian fleets; the largest number of ships were of the small, lightweight variety used for fishing, local trade and transport.

These smaller ships were vital to travel around the Viking homeland countries and of paramount importance to their development. The eleventh-century author Adam of Bremen reported that an overland journey between lower Denmark and upper Sweden would take a month to complete, but only five days by sea.

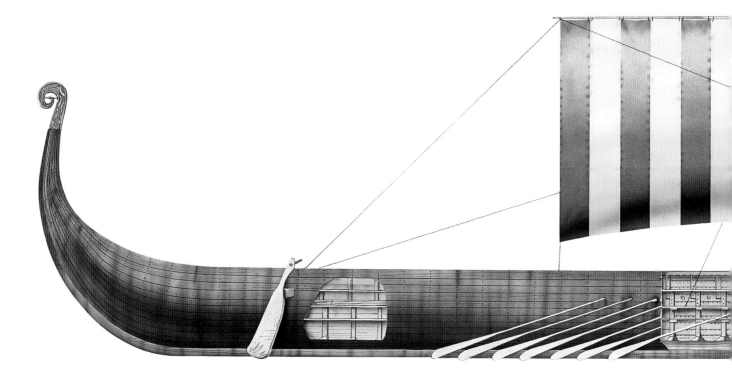

Above: A cutaway reveals the construction of a longship. The long strakes along the ship's sides were built up one by one and riveted together. Once the strakes reached the correct height the crossbeams and other pieces of framework were added.

Trade between the countries was also opened up by the emergence of the market towns of Kaupang, Birka and Hedeby, which were built with quays for easy access by boat. As the towns expanded, so did their harbours and the ships sailing into them: bigger quays were built to berth the larger ships from within Scandinavia and beyond. Overseas traders were not the only ones attracted to these bustling Scandinavian emporia: pirates aboard warships with sails made short work of heavy transport ships laden with goods for sale at nearby markets.

To deter pirates from raiding the market towns themselves, blockades were placed in the water around their harbours; only locals and friendly captains would know the safe route through. These blockades were made from large stone piles, wooden stakes and scuttled ships that had

reached the end of their lives. One such blockade was made in Denmark's Roskilde Fjord on the island of Zealand. Little is known about Roskilde, but Adam of Bremen claimed King Harald Bluetooth was buried there, and the number of ships sunk in the Fjord's narrowest point – a channel known as Skuldelev – indicates it was an important place that needed to be defended. The five ships excavated from the so-called "Skuldelev blockade" have provided a wealth of archeological information about Viking ships and the way they were built.

The *Skuldelev 2* warship found in the Skuldelev blockade is a typical example of the sleek and speedy vessels that were used to take warriors on raids throughout Europe. Around 29m (95ft) long and 4m (13ft) wide, *Skuldelev 2* was built with 30 oar ports on either side to support a crew of 60 men.

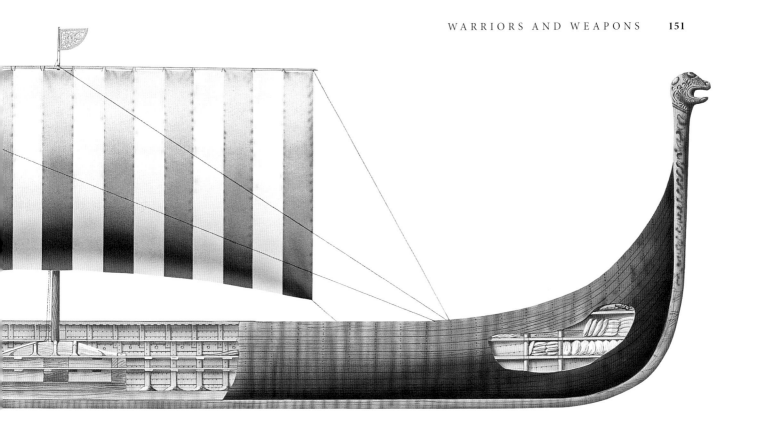

"There were many involved: some to fell, some to carve it, some forging nails, some carrying timber ... the ship was both long and broad and high-sided and large-timbered."

— *Heimskringla*

The construction of the *Skuldelev 2* is representative of all Viking longships. It was made from a clinker-built hull of overlapping strakes, joined with iron rivets and made watertight with animal hair and pitch. The hull had a tapering prow and stern, and was reinforced with crossbeams. Like all Viking ships, the *Skuldelev 2* was built from strakes taken from logs split lengthways, rather than sawn. This gave the strakes a more desirable strength, lightness and flexibility when fitted together to make the finished vessel. A large steering oar would have been fitted to the right side of the *Skuldelev 2*'s stern, and an iron anchor was used to keep it in place.

The *Skuldelev 2* would have had a square or rectangular sail, measuring around 110m^2 (1184ft^2), and a prow perhaps featuring iron curls or a creature's head, such as a dragon, carved from wood. A deck would have run the length of the ship and the Vikings would

Above: The longship fitted with shields and dragon-head prows provides the enduring image of the Viking Age.

have hung their shields from the ship's side. With its striped sail, prow's head, shields and bearded warriors onboard, the *Skuldelev 2* sailing fast towards shore would have been a formidable sight; a fierce, technological terror for the Medieval age.

Warships were only one type of sea-going Viking vessel. *Skuldelev 1*, also from the Skuldelev blockade, was a 16m- (52ft-) long, 4.5m- (15ft-) wide cargo ship built to carry around 24 tons of goods. Its sail would have been around 100m^2 (1076ft^2) and, like all Viking cargo ships, it would not have had oars; a crew of five to eight men could have sailed the ship. The draught of *Skuldelev 1* was around 125cm (49in), which is more than the warships of the time that often had draughts

of around 85cm (33in). The draught is the depth of a loaded vessel taken from the level of the waterline and the ship's lowest point. Those ships with shallower draughts needed less water to float, making them ideal for river raids or beach landings.

Viking ships navigated by hugging the coasts of the countries they were sailing around, but little is known about how they found their way across open ocean. It is thought the Vikings used the position of the Sun, and maybe the stars, to help find their way, but this does not explain what they did when the sky was overcast. When taking long sea voyages, Viking adventurers must have understood they were embarking on a voyage into the unknown: losing their way opened new

Above: *Skuldelev 1* was an 16-metre (52-ft) long cargo ship built from pine and oak in Norway around 1030 CE. It was excavated from the Roskilde Fjord in 1962.

"King Harald made for Thorir's ship, knowing him to be a terrible berserk, and very brave. The fighting was desperate on either side."

— *Grettir's Saga*

opportunities for exploration.

While many long Viking journeys ended up in far-flung countries such as Greenland, America and Russia, others must have been badly blown off course, shipwrecked or lost without a trace. Those family members who stayed at home could only wait, wonder and hope for the return of their sea-going men. Others would be left to ponder the possible reasons they did not come back. A runestone from Nylars Church on the Danish island of Bornholm marks such an incident:

> "Sasser erected this stone to his father Halvard; he drowned at sea with all his crew. Holy Christ have mercy on his soul. May this stone be longlasting."

Roskilde 6

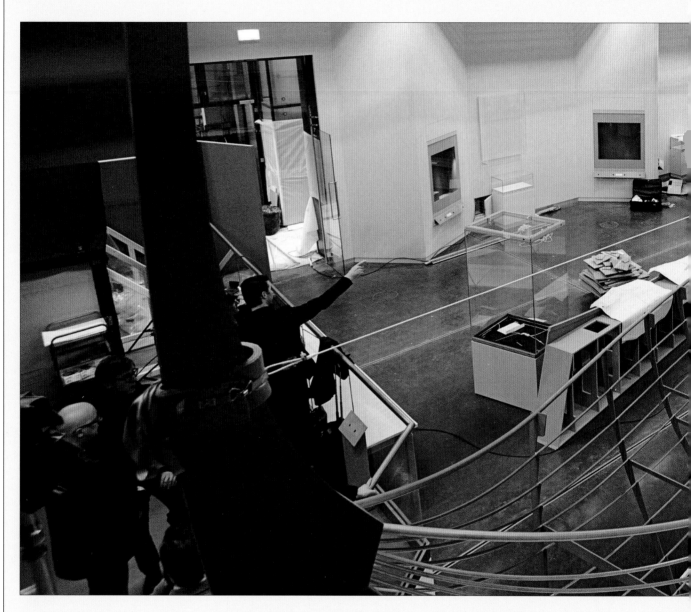

The longest Viking warship ever discovered was the *Roskilde 6*, excavated with the other ships in the Skuldelev blockade. *Roskilde 6* was 37m (121ft) long, 4m (13ft) wide, made from oak – the strongest wood used for Viking ships – and had a draught of 84cm (33in). The ship had 40 pairs of oars for a crew of 80 and was built with one purpose in mind: the transportation of a large force of warriors able to travel far up rivers and land quickly on any shore.

A warship as impressive as *Roskilde 6* could only have been commissioned by a wealthy jarl or king, and the owner of the vessel has been the cause of much speculation since its excavation began in 1996. Using dendrochronology, or the dating of timber from the growth rate of its rings, *Roskilde 6* was thought to have been built between 1018 and 1032. This would place it in a period where Olaf Haraldson was the King of Norway and Cnut the King of England and Denmark. Olaf had been raiding in England until 1015, when he returned to Norway to claim the throne. However, Olaf also declared war on Cnut in 1025, after the English King declared he should also rule over Norway. A naval battle followed

in 1028 near the settlement of Skåne, which all but wiped out the Norwegian king's fleet. Because Olaf's campaign against Cnut started as an amphibious affair, it is possible he commissioned *Roskilde 6* to help with this fight. On the other hand, it could have built by Cnut after his naval success over Olaf.

It is likely *Roskilde 6* belonged to one of these proud Viking kings,

although we may never know for sure. Nor do we know when this great warship was dragged out into the Skuldelev channel and sent to the bottom to block the passage of hostile attackers. It is likely the order to scuttle *Roskilde 6* came from one of the next generation of Danish kings: Cnut's son Harthacnut, who ruled from 1035 to 1042, or Olaf's son Magnus, who ruled from 1042 to 1047.

Above: *Roskilde 6* **is the largest Viking warship ever found and may have belonged to King Olaf Haraldson or King Cnut. It is housed today in the Viking Ship Museum, Roskilde.**

Exploration and Expansion

The Vikings were not only raiders and invaders: they were also explorers, settlers and colonizers. The Swedish Vikings sailed east across the Baltic Sea and beyond, where they built a series of trading settlements along the great rivers of Russia. The Norwegian Vikings went west, undertaking epic sea voyages to the little-known Faeroe Islands, Iceland and Greenland. From there it was only one small hop to the continent undiscovered by Europeans: America.

T he Viking adventures across the Atlantic were born out of necessity rather than a desire for aggressive expansion. In Norway there was only a finite amount of arable land to distribute among its swelling population. Ambitious warriors wishing to lay claim to their own slice of farmland would have to look abroad to new lands in the west.

During the raids of the early ninth century, Norwegian Vikings attacked the native populations of the northern and western Scottish Isles and settled in places not yet inhabited by the locals. They soon overran the islands of Orkney and Shetland, and then the remote,

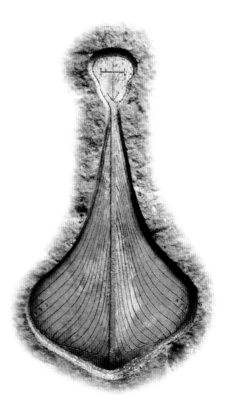

windswept islands around 290km
(180 miles) to the northwest: the
Faeroes. However, the Vikings
were not the first settlers to land
on the 18 volcanic islands that
make up the Faeroes – Irish monks
had lived there as hermits for
many decades.

The monks were the original
explorers of the North Atlantic;
they had sailed into voluntary
exile for God with nothing but
blind faith that they would be
delivered safely somewhere to do
his bidding. A treatise in 825 CE
by the Irish monk Dicuil describes
the Faeroes:

> "[A] set of small islands,
> nearly all separated by narrow
> stretches of water; in these for
> nearly a hundred years hermits
> sailing from our country,
> Ireland, have lived. But just as
> they were always deserted from
> the beginning of the world, so
> now because of the Northman
> pirates they are emptied of
> anchorites, and are filled with
> countless sheep and very many
> diverse kinds of seabirds."
> – Dicuil, *De Mensura Orbis Terrae*,
> translated by J.J. Tierney

The Faeroe monks did not fancy
staying to break bread with the
pagan colonizers, although they
did leave their livestock behind.
The Vikings named their new
home "Færeyjar", or "Sheep
Islands" and began building the
turf and stone longhouses that
lay at the centre of their new
farming communities along the

coast. They soon discovered the Faeroes were also a convenient midway point between the British Isles and a land the Irish monks referred to as "Thule", later to become known as Iceland.

ICELAND

Dicuil described Thule as a land notable for the absence of darkness during summer, when "whatever task a man wishes to perform, even to picking the lice from his shirt, he can manage as precisely as in broad daylight." However, as with the Faeroes, the monks did not wish to share Iceland with the "heathen men" and departed for more Christian homelands. The Vikings themselves did not at first take to the new land of Thule, which they discovered entirely by accident in around 860.

Garðar Svavarsson was the first Viking to be blown off course and onto the shores of Iceland while

trying to reach the Hebrides. Garðar circumnavigated the island, overwintered there, named it "Garðarshólm" and then sailed away. The next accidental arrival was Naddod, who was trying to sail from Norway to the Faeroes. He renamed Thule "Snæland", or "Snowland", but didn't stay. Instead, a Viking called Flóki Vilgerðarson travelled deliberately to Iceland to explore its barren, volcanic shores. Flóki loaded his large cargo ship with livestock, men and building equipment and intended to settle permanently on the island. He soon changed his mind.

Flóki's plan was to use three ravens to help him find a promising piece of land by releasing them and following them to shore if they did not return to the ship. Finally, one of the birds did not return and Flóki followed its path to Vatnsfjörð in northwestern Iceland. Here, Flóki's ship became iced-in and

Facing page: The excavated remains of a tenth-century longhouse, discovered in the town of Leirvík, Eysturoy Island, the Faroe Islands.

Below: This romanticised early twentieth-century illustration shows the Vikings approaching the shores of Iceland.

Icelandic Farms

Above: A reconstruction of the Stöng Farmhouse in southern Iceland.

Ingólf's farmhouse on the original site of Reykjavik was typical of the settlements of Iceland. These followed the standard long-hall design and were built from stone, timber and turf, with one or two ancillary rooms added to the ends. The main room was often large – some were more than 40m (131ft) long – and were used for feasts and pagan festivals. There were no towns or villages in Iceland before the thirteenth century, and the great hall of a goðar would have served as the central gathering place for a local community.

One of the most famous Icelandic farmsteads is the Stöng Farmhouse in the Thjórsárdalur Valley in southern Iceland. The farmhouse was preserved by a layer of volcanic ash until its excavation in 1939, and has provided unique insights into the daily lives of Icelandic Vikings. The main room of the farmhouse was 17m (56ft) long with raised sleeping platforms and a central hearth. A smaller living room, also with a central hearth, was probably used for spinning, and two ancillary rooms were used for a toilet and

for storage – probably of fish, which made up the mainstay of the Icelandic diet. Outhouses served as a barn and smithy, where bog iron ore was found ready to be forged. The Stöng Farmhouse was abandoned suddenly in 1104 when the nearby Hekla volcano erupted and ash covered half the island. This was a catastrophic event that rendered many of Iceland's farms useless. However, the threat of volcanic activity was part of life on Iceland and the Viking communities still managed to thrive.

the pioneer was trapped for a long, harsh winter. Flóki survived, but his livestock starved to death. Cold and disappointed, the explorer returned to Norway the next spring to vent furiously about a land he rechristened "Iceland".

The name stuck, although others were not put off by Flóki's bitter accounts, and from 870

the first Norse settlers arrived in Iceland. According to the twelfth-century *Landnámabók*, the so-called "First Settler of Iceland" was a warrior called Ingólf Arnarson, who sailed from Norway with a ship laden heavy with his family, livestock and worldly goods to inhabit a place he called "Reykjavik", or "Steamy Bay".

Ingólf was a typical emigrant risking all for a new life abroad. He had fallen out with the local chieftains in Norway and wanted to set up a new independent republic far from the tyranny of Norway's King Harald Finehair. Those fleeing King Harald's rule were mostly browbeaten aristocrats who arrived in Iceland with retinues of warriors and thralls and laid claim to the country's choicest parcels of arable land. These aristocrats became the goði: priest-chieftains of Iceland who ruled over their local districts and settled disputes at local Things.

Around 40 goði would meet annually at the national Althing, held at Thingvellir, a large, long gash in the rocky landscape banked by a wall of solidified lava. The Althing has often been hailed as the first early medieval democracy: everything from common laws, to the calling of holmgang duels, and the 1000 CE introduction of Christianity were passed at the Althing. The republic of Iceland managed to govern itself under the laws of the Althing and escape the interference of royal rule until it was taken over by Norway in 1263.

EIRIK THE RED AND GREENLAND

Blood feuds, storms, the threat of volcanic eruption and the growing scarcity of land were the forces that drove Icelandic Vikings to new shores to the north west. Greenland had been discovered accidentally around 930, when seafarer Gunnbjorn Ulf-Krakason was blown off course and washed past a hostile, mountainous, icy landmass. This was the same land that Norwegian Viking Eirik the Red decided to colonize.

Eirik the Red, so-called for either his ruddy complexion or his hot temper, was a violent troublemaker who left his home in southwestern Norway "because of some killings" according to his eponymous saga. He moved to Iceland around 960, but found the island was full up with little land left for latecomers. Eirik eventually married into a wealthy family who gave him his own piece of land to farm. However, trouble was never far away from Eirik: one day, his thralls caused a landslide that flattened his neighbour's house; weapons were drawn and a blood feud ensued. Eirik tried to escape the violence by moving to the remote Suðurey Island in the southwest, but then there was another dispute with a neighbour, followed this time by a pitched battle. The largely tolerant frontier community in Iceland outlawed

> *"People would be the more eager to go there if it had a good name."*
>
> — *Eirik the Red*

Eirik for three years. He had to leave immediately or face lawful execution by anyone who fancied their luck.

Eirik's following sea voyage took him around Cape Farwell at Greenland's most southern point to the island's west, where he set up camp. Greenland was a land of extremes: at the foot of the inhospitable icecap that takes up the bulk of the interior were sheltered fjords, green strips of land and an abundance of seafood. After his three-year exile, Eirik returned to Iceland in 985 in a boat loaded with exotic goods, including seal hides, bearskins and walrus ivory. These, Eirik told the amazed Icelanders, came from the rich and prosperous country of "Greenland" – for, as Eirik reasoned in the sagas, "people

Above: An artistic rendering of Eirik the Red landing on the shores of Greenland. As "first settler" of the new Viking colony, Eirik was able to enjoy special status.

Facing page, top right: The remains of Eirik the Red's farmhouse at Brattahlid, in the Eastern Settlement of Greenland. The farmhouse overlooks Eirikfjord.

Facing page, bottom right: A map showing the sea voyages to and from the Viking colony of Greenland and the North Atlantic territories where their artefacts have been found.

would be the more eager to go there if it had a good name".

It was a clever turn. In 986, Eirik set sail from Iceland once again, this time at the head of a fleet of 25 ships laden with around 300 pioneers and their belongings. For many, it was to be their last voyage; only 14 ships actually made it to Greenland. Some were sent to the bottom by a freak wave; others turned back to Iceland to escape the storm.

Those who reached Greenland quickly discovered the icy reality behind the enticing name, but there was worse news: evidence of another people already inhabiting the island. These were indigenous Inuits that the Vikings called "skrælings", which translates roughly as "wretches". The skrælings mostly inhabited the

north of Greenland, where they lived according to the traditions of a Stone-Age culture and survived by fishing from hide-covered canoes. The skrælings and Vikings were to have an erratic relationship that veered between friendliness and hostility, but that did not stop the Vikings' settlement of the new country. The pioneers broke into two groups, founding the Eastern Settlement under Eirik on the southwestern coast above Cape Farwell, and the Western Settlement around 644km (400 miles) along the coast to the north.

Eirik enjoyed the power and prestige afforded to the "First Settler" in the same way Ingólf Arnarson had done in Iceland a century before: he built the first farm at Brattahlid and took the role of the Law Speaker at the Greenland Thing. Greenland was also settled in more or less the same way as Iceland. At its peak there were 190 farms in the Eastern Settlement, 90 farms in the Western Settlement and a population of between 3000 and 4000 people. There were also 16 churches, as in 1000 CE Greenland became a Christian country. This was due to Eirik's son Leif Eiriksson, who was converted by King Olaf Tryggvason on his travels to Norway and brought the religion back with him. The *Saga of Eirik the Red* records Leif's homecoming:

"Leif reached land in Eiriksfjordr, and proceeded home to Brattahlid. The people received him gladly. He soon after preached Christianity and Catholic truth throughout the land, making known to the people the message of King Olaf Tryggvason; and declaring how many renowned deeds and what great glory accompanied this faith. Eirik took coldly to the proposal to forsake his religion, but his wife, Thjodhild, promptly yielded, and caused a church to be built not very near the houses. The building was called Thjodhild's Church; in that spot she offered her prayers, and so did those men who received Christ, and they were many. After she accepted the faith, Thjodhild would have no intercourse with Eirik, and this was a great trial to his temper."

– *Saga of Eirik the Red*, translated by J. Sephton

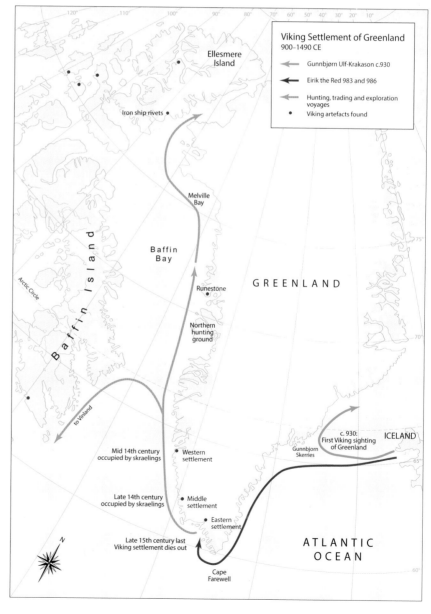

Viking Settlement of Greenland
900–1490 CE

Gunnbjørn Ulf-Krakason c.930

Eirik the Red 983 and 986

Hunting, trading and exploration voyages

Viking artefacts found

Ellesmere Island

Iron ship rivets

Melville Bay

Baffin Island

Baffin Bay

Arctic Circle

Runestone

GREENLAND

Northern hunting ground

to Vinland

Mid 14th century occupied by skraelings

Western settlement

Late 14th century occupied by skraelings

Middle settlement

Eastern settlement

Late 15th century last Viking settlement dies out

Cape Farewell

c. 930: First Viking sighting of Greenland

ICELAND

Gunnbjorn Skerries

ATLANTIC OCEAN

N

Above: The interior of Eirik the Red's reconstructed farmhouse at Brattahlid, Greenland. The central hearth and platforms along the walls are typical of Viking longhouses.

Leif Eiriksson became a celebrated figure among his own people on Greenland; his voyage to America added to his fame. According to the *Saga of the Greenlanders*, this new land was first sighted by Bjarni Herjólfsson, who, in the Viking tradition associated with North Atlantic sea travel, was blown off course and lost in the fog while trying to reach Greenland from Iceland in 986. When the fog lifted, Bjarni found himself sailing alongside an unfamiliar forested shore. Unconvinced that he was in the right country, Bjarni forbade his crew from landing, kept close to the coast and miraculously ended up some weeks later in Greenland.

Vinland Grapes

Bjarni's stories about this strange new country convinced Leif Eiriksson to pick up the trail. Leif and his crew of 35 warriors first encountered a land of glaciers, mountains and flat slabs of rock, which he called "Helluland" ("Slab Land"). Sailing south, he came to the forested shores described by Bjarni, which he called "Markland", or "Wood Land", and gave the order to land. This brief visit marked the first known European footfall on the continent of America. Leif and his men then sailed further south to a flat, grassy landscape where they built buðir, or "booths", a type of temporary shelter and overwintered there.

Two things about the new

land amazed the Viking visitors: the frost-free mornings, and a sun that stayed in the sky all day from morning until the afternoon. Another discovery gave the new country its name. This came from a German called Tyrkir, who returned late one day with a scouting party. To the amusement of his Scandinavian shipmates, Tyrkir was in a highly agitated state, babbling incoherently in his mother tongue about wild grapes – he had even brought back several bunches as evidence. Leif was impressed: grapes were impossible to grow in Iceland or Greenland and any wine drunk was imported. He immediately named this fertile country of plenty "Vinland", or "Wine Land".

Leif did not try to settle in Vinland: instead that fell to a man named Thorfinn Karlsefni who sailed to the new country with 60 men, five women and livestock. Thorfinn found Leif's abandoned booths and remained in Vinland for three years, and looked set to stay there. But he had not reckoned with the indigenous people, described by the sagas as "short men, ill-looking, with their hair in disorderly fashion on their heads; they were large-eyed, and had broad cheeks." The Vikings called these people skrælings, although it is not clear if they were related to the Inuit people of Greenland, or instead Native Americans. Whatever their roots, these locals did not intend to let the Vikings

Above: An artistic impression of Leif Eiriksson's voyage to the east coast of North America in the late tenth century.

Above: The Vikings are attacked by the skrælings of North America. The indigenous people made it impossible for the Vikings to settle in the new land.

stay in their country. After initial cordial relations, the skrælings began to attack the Viking settlement in increasingly large numbers. Rather than be overrun, Thorfinn and his pioneers sailed regretfully back to Greenland.

Greenland itself also only became a temporary Viking settlement. After falling under the rule of Norway in 1261, the climate began to deteriorate and violent conflict broke out with the skrælings, who were migrating south away from the worsening conditions. Contact was lost with Greenland from 1410, and at that time only the Eastern Settlement had survived. Then, in 1540, a ship visiting the Eastern Settlement found it completely deserted, except for one unburied body lying alone in a longhouse. No-one knows about the final end of the Viking colony of Greenland.

VIKINGS IN THE EAST

While the Norwegian Vikings colonized the lands to the northwest, the Swedish Vikings looked towards more accessible shores in the east. Their subsequent settlements in the Baltic and in Russia were among the oldest and longest surviving in the story of Viking expansion. However, unlike their western counterparts the Swedish Vikings did not base their settlements on a foundation of raiding and invading, but on trade.

The Swedish Vikings built their first trading towns on the nearby Baltic shores at Grobina, Latvia, as early as 650 CE. From Grobina it was a short journey northwest across open water to the market town of Birka; it also provided a good stopping point between Sweden and what is now St Petersburg in the northeast. From

L'Anse aux Meadows

Above: The reconstructed turf buildings at L'Anse aux Meadows, Newfoundland, including a 24 metre - (78ft-) long longhouse.

There has been much speculation about exactly where the Vikings landed along the east coast of America, known to them as Vinland. It is thought Helluland was probably Baffin Island; Markland was probably Labrador. The only solid evidence of a Viking settlement in America has been found at L'Anse aux Meadows on the northern tip of Newfoundland. Here, large turf-walled buildings similar to those found in Iceland and Greenland have been discovered alongside Scandinavian objects that include a spindle whorl, a fastening pin and a bone knitting needle. A furnace was also found with iron objects such as nails, rivets and a buckle, that were typically forged by a Viking smithy. Evidence shows the settlement at L'Anse aux Meadows was used only for a short time, which corresponds to the dates of Viking exploration found in the sagas. But despite this tantalizing evidence there is no absolute proof that the settlement belonged to the Vikings.

here, the small trading settlement of Staraya Ladoga could be reached by the Volkhov River. Staraya Ladoga was founded by local Slavic tribes on the banks of the Volkhov around 750. It soon became a bustling, multi-ethnic community and meeting-point for trade; here silver Arabic dirhams from the east were exchanged for Viking furs and slaves from the west.

The Vikings did not see Staraya Ladoga as a target for a hit-and-run raid, but more as a long-term business opportunity. Silver dirhams were one of the most valuable commodities of the Viking world, and large hoards of the coins discovered on the Swedish island of Gotland as well as Staraya Ladoga attest to the wealth of the eastern Vikings trading in them. It is little wonder that many of these same Vikings decided not just to visit Staraya Ladoga on trading jaunts, but to settle there, trade in dirhams and exact tributes from

Above: A map showing Viking incursions in eastern Europe in the eighth and ninth centuries. During this time, the Vikings raided along the river networks of Russia, founded Kievan Rus, and attacked and traded with Constantinople.

Facing page: An impression by Russian artist Nicholas Roerich depicts the Viking Rus travelling down the perilous river networks towards Constantinople.

the local tribes. They became known as the Rus, which roughly translates as the "Men Who Row". From Staraya Ladoga, the Rus moved further south down the river networks and set up trading bases at Novgorod, Gnezdovo and Kiev. This became the heart of an early Russian state, which took its name from the Vikings who settled there – the Rus.

The earliest written source about the Rus is the twelfth century *Russian Primary Chronicle*. It begins with the Vikings' banishment from the Russian region by local tribes who were tired of having to pay them tributes. However, once the Rus (or Varangians, as they were also known) were gone, anarchy ensued:

"These are the tales of bygone years regarding the origin of the land of Rus, the first princes of Kiev and how the land of Rus had its beginning... 860–862: The four tribes who had been forced to pay tribute to the Varangians drove them back beyond the sea, refused to pay them further tribute and set out to govern themselves. But there was no law among them, and tribe rose against tribe. Discord thus followed among them, and they began to war one against the other. They said to themselves, 'Let us seek a prince who may rule

"They harry the Slavs, using ships to reach them, they carry them off as slaves and sell them to the Khazars and Bulgars."

— Ibn Rustah

over us, and judge us according to custom'. Thus they went overseas to the Varangians, to the Rus... then said to the Rus, 'Our land is great and rich, but there is no order in

it. Come reign as princes, rule over us'. Three brothers, with their kinfolk, were selected. They brought with them all the Rus and migrated. The oldest, Rurik, located himself in

Above: Found on Gotland, this runestone depicts a ship of Odin carrying the souls of warrior heroes killed in battle to the afterworld.

Facing page: A bronze brooch discovered in a tenth-century Viking burial mound in Gnezdovo, Smolensk Oblast, Russia.

Novgorod; the second, Sineus, in Beloozero; and the third, Truvor, in Izborsk. From these Varangians, the Russian land received its name."
  – *Russian Primary Chronicle*, translated by S.H. Cross and O.P. Sherbowitz-Wetzor

Now legitimized as the rulers of trading settlements that stretched from Staraya Ladoga to Novgorod and Kiev, the Vikings controlled the local tribes by force or alliance, exacting tribute and doing business. Novgorod, ruled over by Rurik, became an important centre point in the lands now dominated by the Rus, a junction between the great Russian rivers, the Volkhov, the Dvina, the Dnieper and the Volga. The Volga could be followed to the Caspian Sea and beyond into central Asia; the Dnieper led to the Black Sea and the Danube.

The size and manoeuvrability of the Vikings ships was vital for travel down the river networks. These were not the great sea-going vessels that helped the Vikings colonize the islands of Iceland and Greenland, but instead smaller, lighter craft that could be picked out of the water and dragged overland when the need arose. This method of transport, known as portage, was time-consuming and cumbersome, and wholly necessary where there was a gap between two rivers or the build-up of ice made it impossible to pass.

Sailing to the Great City

The Vikings were never ones for staying put. In 860, a group of Kiev Vikings sailed as far south as Constantinople – or Miklagarðr, "The Great City", as they called it. Constantinople, the capital of the Byzantium Empire, was indeed a great city: as bridge between east and west it had a cosmopolitan population of around 500,000 people and the largest markets

The Rus

Portage was just one aspect of Viking methods that made a lasting impression on the startled people of the east. The Persian geographer Ibn Rustah encountered the Rus on his travels down the River Volga and wrote the following account in the tenth century:

"As for the Rus, they live on an island... that takes three days to walk round and is covered with thick undergrowth and forests...

They harry the Slavs, using ships to reach them; they carry them off as slaves and sell them to the Khazars and Bulgars. They have no fields but simply live on what they get from the Slav's lands... When a son is born, the father will go up to the newborn baby, sword in hand; throwing it down, he says, 'I shall not leave you with any property: You have only what you can provide using this weapon... They have no villages or estates, or fields. Their only occupation is

trading in martens and squirrel and other kinds of furs... They carry clean clothes and the men adorn themselves with bracelets and gold. They treat their slaves well and also they carry exquisite clothes, because they put great effort in trade. They have many towns. They have a most friendly attitude towards foreigners and strangers who seek refuge."

– Ibn Rustah,
Book of Precious Records,
translated by Michael Jan de Goeje

Above: The extent of the Kievan Rus in 912 at the time of Oleg's death. Under Oleg, the Kievan Rus had become a powerful, consolidated state.

of the known world. Merchants from every corner of every country traded in Constantinople, and the city must have been an irresistible lure for the luxury-hunting Vikings.

But in 860, the Vikings came not to trade but to loot. The people of Constantinople responded hysterically, according to Patriarch Photius, the defender of the city:

"A people has crept down from the north… the people is *fierce* and has no mercy, its voice is as the roaring sea. We have heard reports of them, or rather we have beheld their massed aspect, and our hands have waxed feeble; anguish has seized us, and pangs as a woman in travail."

– *The Homilies of Photius*, translated by Cyril Mango

Photius's account of the panic in Constantinople is difficult to assess. There is little evidence to suggest the Viking attack was as severe as he claimed, but Photius's description is of fevered, wholesale slaughter:

> "They spared nothing… but boldly thrusting their swords through persons of every age and sex. One could see babes torn away by them from breast and milk and finding an improvised grave in the rocks against which they were dashed… Everything was full of dead bodies; the flow of rivers was turned into blood; some of the fountains and reservoirs it was no longer possible to distinguish as their cavities were made level with corpses."
> – *The Homilies of Photius*

Whatever the actual damage, the attack on Constantinople was only the first in a series of raids on the city that invariably ended with a peace treaty and a hefty tribute payment. The next recorded raid came in 907 and was led by Oleg, a relative of Rurik and the new ruler of Novgorod and Kiev. Oleg was reported to have sailed a fleet of 200 ships down the River Dnieper and over the Black Sea, but he then found his way to Constantinople blocked by a large chain strung across the Bosphorus River. Not to be deterred, Oleg ordered his ships portaged past the obstacle and put back in the water.

Once the Vikings were at the gates of Constantinople, a peace treaty was immediately offered to prevent any bloodshed. At first, the treaty stipulated that the warriors could trade in Constantinople, but not stay in the city. Four years later, the deal was amended to include special trading privileges and the right to live in the city for up to six months, something previously

Above: A stylized image of the fabled Varangian Guard standing before the Byzaantine emperor. Viking warriors made up some of the original members of the guard.

Above: A map showing where artefacts of Viking origin have been discovered in eastern Europe.

Facing page: A fifteenth-century impression of Oleg's threatened attack on Constantinople. In the end, the Rus prince was paid off by the emperor and later awarded handsome trading privileges.

afforded only to the Syrians. In return, the Vikings had to send back the large number of Christian slaves taken from Byzantium and agree to prosecution in future for any such crimes. They were also notably given free passes to the Constantinople baths, which can be taken either as a sign of the Vikings' penchant for washing, or their need to begin doing it. It is also interesting that the Vikings

signing the deal had strikingly Scandinavian names – Karli, Ingjald, Farulf, Hrollaf, Vermund – showing that the Rus had not yet become an assimilated part of the indigenous Slavic culture of Russia.

Raiding Byzantium

In 914, Oleg died and his son Igor took his throne at Kiev. Following in his father's footsteps, Igor continued the Viking attacks on

Въ лѣт. Ꙅ. у. аі. Игоревичевъ взрастьшю. и хожаше по Олзѣ и слоушаше ѣ. и приведоша ѣмоу женоу ѿ пьскова. именемь Ѡлено Въ лѣт. Ꙅ. у. ві. Въ лѣт. Ꙅ. у. гі.

Въ лѣт. Ꙅ. у. ді. Въ лѣт. Ꙅ. у. еі. Иде Ѡлегъ на Грекы. и гора ѡставивъ Игорь Києвѣ. поꙗ множество варѧгъ. и слов ень. и чюдь. и словене. и кривичи. и мерю. и деревлѧ ны. и радимичи. и полѧны. и сѣверо. и вѧтичи. и хо рваты. и доулѣбы. и тиверци. ꙗже соуть толко вины. си вси звахоуть ѿ грекъ великаꙗ скоуѳ. съ сими со всѣми поиде Ѡлегъ на конихъ и на кораблѣ. и бѣ число мъ кораблен. в. прииде къ цѣсарюградоу. и греци замкоша соудъ. а градъ затвориша ∴

И выиде Ѡлегъ на брегъ. и воевати нача много оу бииства сотвори. ѿколо града грькомъ и разбиша многы полаты. и по ожгоша цьркви. а нихъже има хоу плѣнникы. ѡвѣхъ посѣкахоу дроугиꙗ же моу чахоу. иныꙗ же растрелахоу. а дроугыꙗ амореꙗ метахоу. и ина многа творѧхоу роусь грекомъ. елико же ратнии творѧть ∴

> *"They spared nothing... but boldly thrusting their swords through persons of every age and sex."*
>
> — *Patriarch Photius*

Above: A coin depicting Byzantine Emperor Constantine VII Porphyrogenitus, who lived from 905 to 959.

the Byzantine Empire in a series of raids on its towns around the Black Sea. This gave the Vikings their introduction to "Greek fire", a type of petroleum gel that could be pumped from tubes or thrown in canisters like hand grenades. The weapon was devastatingly effective against Igor's fleet; most of his men were either burned alive or drowned while trying to escape. According to the *Russian Primary Chronicle*, Igor's improbably large fleet of 10,000 was reduced to only a dozen ships as the Vikings limped home.

Igor returned with another fleet in 944, and this time he was simply bought off by Emperor Constantine VII Porphyrogenitus, who wished to prevent any further casualties on his watch. The following treaty, which accompanied Porphyrogenitus's large tribute, stipulated that the Vikings would have to declare how many ships they wished to bring into Constantinople in the future. They would also be restricted in the amount of silk they bought in the city, and were no longer allowed to overwinter at the mouth of the Dnieper River. This last clause was a canny move by Porphyrogenitus: the rivers were perilous after the winter snow had thawed and the emperor knew it.

In his *De Administrando Imperio*, written as a foreign policy guide for his son and successor Romanus II, Porphyrogenitus explains the hazardous journey undertaken by the Vikings to Constantinople and the pitfalls associated with it. They included an 80-km (50-mile) section of river rapids that could be tackled only by first unloading the ships and then navigating them

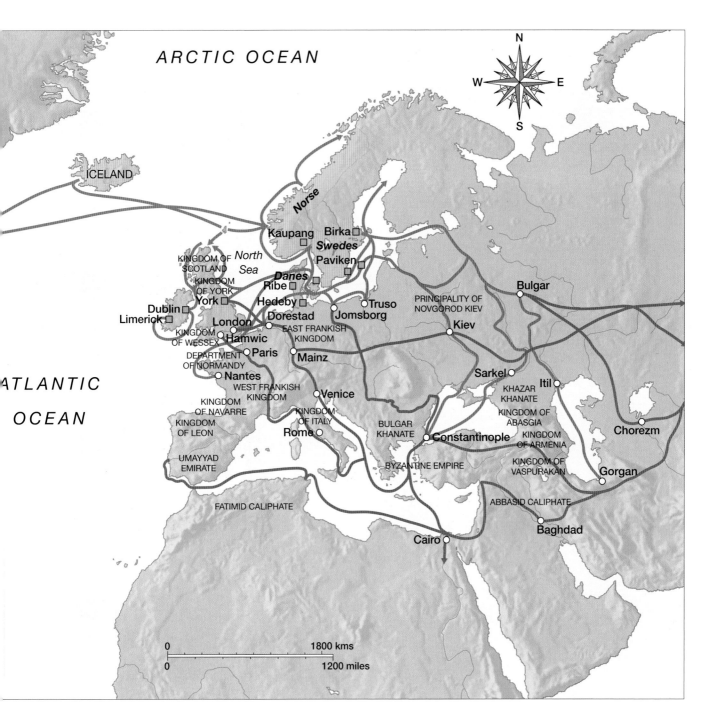

ARCTIC OCEAN

N
W E
S

ICELAND

ATLANTIC OCEAN

Norse

Kaupang
Birka
Swedes
Paviken

North Sea

KINGDOM OF SCOTLAND
KINGDOM OF YORK

Danes
Ribe
Hedeby
Dorestad
Truso
Jomsborg

PRINCIPALITY OF NOVGOROD KIEV

Bulgar

Dublin
Limerick
York
London
Hamwic
KINGDOM OF WESSEX
EAST FRANKISH KINGDOM
Kiev

DEPARTMENT OF NORMANDY
Paris
Mainz

Nantes
WEST FRANKISH KINGDOM
Venice

Sarkel
Itil
KHAZAR KHANATE

KINGDOM OF NAVARRE

KINGDOM OF LEON
KINGDOM OF ITALY
Rome

BULGAR KHANATE
Constantinople

KINGDOM OF ABASGIA
KINGDOM OF ARMENIA

Chorezm

UMAYYAD EMIRATE

BYZANTINE EMPIRE

KINGDOM OF VASPURAKAN
Gorgan

FATIMID CALIPHATE

ABBASID CALIPHATE
Baghdad

Cairo

0   1800 kms
0   1200 miles

by Vikings holding long poles. Further on, these rapids – given names by the Vikings such as "The Yeller", "The Laugher" and "The Drinker" – became impassable and the boats had to be portaged across land to a calmer section of water. A further danger was ambush by the local Slavic tribe known as the "Pechenegs". The way to Constantinople was a fraught and

perilous journey, and without the option of overwintering it lost its appeal for Igor.

Caspian Adventures

Instead, the ruler of Kiev decided to target the relatively untested coastal Caspian Sea settlements belonging to the Khazars, Bulgars and Arabs. Securing these trade routes would ensure a larger share

Above: A map showing the extent of the Vikings' influence in the world. During the Viking Age, Scandinavian warriors travelled tremendous distances, spanning from the Caspian Sea in the east, to the Atlantic coast of North America in the west.

Above: Vladimir made a show of renouncing the Viking pagan gods and converting to Christianity. The Rus leader was later made a saint.

an attack by Azerbaijan warriors. Those managing to escape under cover of darkness kept only a token amount of their plundered loot.

Igor died soon afterwards and was replaced by his son Svyatoslav, the first of the Rus to be given a Slavic name. However, Viking blood ran through Svyatoslav's veins: he attacked the Byzantines and then waged war against the Khazars, destroying their towns around the Caspian Sea and the capital at Itil. Next, Svyatoslav targeted the Bulgars along the River Danube, a successful campaign at first until a new Byzantine Emperor John I Tzimiskes took the Bulgars' side in 971 and all but destroyed the warring Rus. Limping home to Kiev, Svyatoslav was finally attacked by the Pechenegs, who reportedly decapitated the Viking and used his skull as a cup.

Assimilation

Svyatoslav's successor was his son Vladimir, and his rule marks the point where Kievan Rus changed from being a Viking trading settlement to a Slavic kingdom. After taking the throne at Kiev, Vladimir converted to Christianity and made a show of renouncing the Viking pagan gods. Vladimir viewed his heritage as something of an embarrassment. In the past, the rulers of the Kievan Rus had welcomed Viking mercenaries from Scandinavia, but now they served only as a reminder to Vladimir of his brutish origins. Vladimir considered himself a respectable Christian leader: he had married the Byzantine emperor Basil II's daughter

of the silver dirhams being mined in the Arabic east. However, Igor's raid on the town of Bardha'a, in modern Azerbaijan, was a disaster. After slaughtering the local population and inhabiting the town for several months, Igor's men fell ill with dysentery and were then devastated during

> ## *"They lift their ships off the river and carry them past by portaging them on their shoulders."*
>
> ### — *Porphyrogenitus*

Anna, and did not want gangs of marauding barbarians making trouble for him. Instead he sent the incoming Viking warriors south to Constantinople, where they became part of his father-in-law's personal bodyguard, known as the "Varangian Guard".

It is likely one of these warriors carved a piece of runic graffiti into a marble banister at the church of Hagia Sophia in Constantinople. Although today only the name "Halfdan" is legible, it is a fair assumption that "Halfdan was here" was the original sentence. It is easy to imagine Halfdan as a member of the Varangian Guard on duty during a boring service at Hagia Sophia scratching away at the marble. The runes left for posterity by Halfdan serve as a reminder that not only he, but the Vikings as a whole, "were here". For over 200 years, the Swedish Vikings had developed their simple trading emporia into large towns, and then carried on the great Viking traditions of raiding, subjugating the local people and building fierce and lasting reputations.

But by the mid-eleventh century it was all over: the pagan gods had been replaced with Christian ones and the Kievan Rus leaders had become more Slavic than Scandinavian. The Vikings in the east were gone.

The Decline of the Vikings

In the 980s, after nearly a century of peace, the Vikings began a final burst of attacks on Britain. This was no rabble of opportunistic raiders, but professional armies organized to butcher and blackmail. At Maldon in Essex, "The wolvish Vikings, avid for slaughter… hurled their spears, hard as files, and sent sharp darts flying from their hands. Bow strings were busy, shields parried point. Bitter was the battle. Brave men fell on both sides."

T he Battle of Maldon, so vividly described above, occurred around Northey Island at the head of the Blackwater River. In 991 a large Viking army had sailed up the river and encamped on Northey Island, awaiting the Anglo-Saxon response from the nearby town of Maldon.

A force was presently dispatched, led by Earl Byrhtnoth, who drew up by a tidal causeway that separated the island from the mainland. As it was high tide, a Viking herald called out terms across the water to the Anglo-Saxons: they would offer a truce in exchange for cash, or otherwise suffer the consequences.

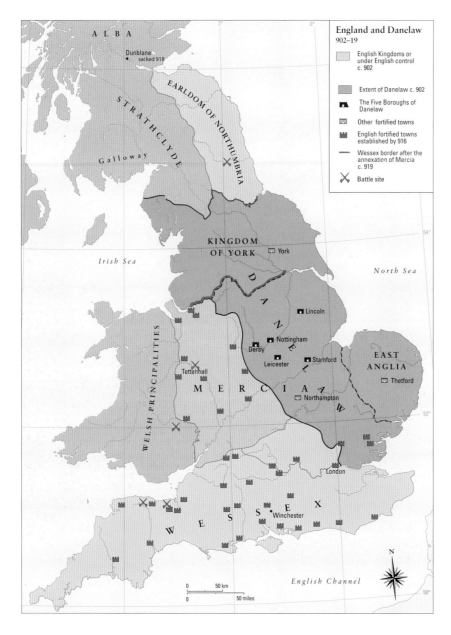

England and Danelaw
902–19

▨ English Kingdoms or
under English control
c. 902

▨ Extent of Danelaw c. 902

🏰 The Five Boroughs of
Danelaw

🏯 Other fortified towns

🏰 English fortified towns
established by 916

— Wessex border after the
annexation of Mercia
c. 919

✕ Battle site

Previous page - main image: An artistic impression of the 991 Battle of Maldon. The bridge, the horned helmets and the Viking kite shields are a few of the historically incorrect embellishments.

Previous page - inset image: A statue of the doomed Anglo-Saxon Earl Byrhtnoth, whose "pride of heart" cost him dearly.

Byrhtnoth snorted at this. The causeway was only 1.8m (6ft) wide – even at low tide – making an all-out Viking assault untenable. Instead their warriors would have to cross in single file. This would also give Byrhtnoth time to wait for reinforcements: he had 500 men with him, around a fifth of the Viking force. Confident, Byrhtnoth shouted back his reply: "We will pay you with spear tips and sword blades."

Byrhtnoth's message was not well received. Leading the

Vikings was none other than Olaf Tryggvason, a Norwegian noble who claimed royal lineage to King Harald Finehair. He was not going to be denied his prize. As the tide began to ebb, Olaf ordered his archers to fire a volley and then sent a handful of men charging across the now exposed causeway. In response, Byrhtnoth commanded three of his champions to stand and guard the end of the causeway. The strategy worked: the Vikings could not pass.

Seeing the day would not be won by brute force alone, Olaf decided to appeal to Byrhtnoth's sense of chivalry and bravado. He called out to the Anglo-Saxon leader, asking permission for his army to cross the causeway, so the two sides could battle like honourable warriors. According to "The Battle of Maldon" poem, Byrhtnoth was "overswayed by his pride of heart" and agreed to the Viking terms.

It was a catastrophic decision that cost Byrhtnoth the battle – and his life. After letting the Vikings cross the causeway, the Anglo-Saxons tried to stop their charge with a shield wall, but they were overwhelmed and forced to fight man-to-man in a brutal mêlée. Byrhtnoth was fatally wounded by a flying spear, and had to be later buried with a ball of wax for a head after his dead body was decapitated. In the confusion following Byrhtnoth's death, his men panicked and many fled. Those who remained were cut down by their Viking foe.

In the end, Olaf got what he wanted: money. The English

King Æthelred was advised to pay the warriors off or face more bloodshed. The resulting Danegeld was around 22,000 pounds (9980kg) of silver and gold. It was the first of many payments that would make the Vikings rich and give Æthelred his unfortunate sobriquet "The Unready", more accurately translated as "The Ill-Advised". It was an accurate description of his reign, as Æthelred soon discovered his payments to stop the Vikings hordes only served as encouragement for future attacks.

For the next two decades, the Viking assaults continued in earnest. Olaf Tryggvason was joined by an unlikely ally, King Svein Forkbeard of Denmark, in an attack on London in 994. Although this failed, the pair instead sailed straight for the southern coast of England to harry the communities there. In response, Æthelred paid the Vikings 16,000 pounds (7260kg) of silver to

Above: King Æthelred is here advised by the clergy to pay the Vikings off with a Danegeld – the first of many payments that earned him the unfortunate sobriquet "The Unready".

Facing page: A map showing the Danelaw, a region of England controlled by the Danish Vikings under an 886 agreement made with Alfred the Great. Like Viking Scandinavia, the Danelaw was politically fragmented and it was not destined to last. By the mid-tenth century the Anglo-Saxons had won the territory back.

The Jelling Dynasty

Svein Forkbeard belonged to a long line of Danish kings known as the Jelling Dynasty. In the tenth century, Svein's father King Harald Bluetooth had been responsible for starting the centralization of power in the Viking homelands. He was helped in this task by his conversion to Christianity, making him a divinely ordained king under Christ. After coming to the Danish throne in 958, Harald also became king of Norway for a period in 970.

Harald celebrated his reign by building a royal monument at the seat of his kingdom in Jelling, Denmark. This consisted of a church, two burial mounds and a runestone to go alongside one previously erected by his father Gorm. The two runestones herald Denmark's transition from a pagan kingdom into a Christian one, and are today proudly associated with Denmark's evolution into a nation state. The older runestone, erected by King Gorm, reads: "King Gormr made this monument in memory of Thyrvé, his wife, Denmark's adornment." Harald Bluetooth's runestone depicted Jesus Christ disentangling himself from a thorn bush, meant to symbolize the emergence of Christianity from the

Above: The Jelling runestones, which symbolize Denmark's transition from paganism to Christianity.

old pagan beliefs. The runestone reads: "King Haraldr ordered this monument made in memory of Gormr, his father, and in memory of Thyrvé, his mother; that Haraldr who won for himself all of Denmark and Norway and made the Danes Christian."

Harald's conversion, however, did not make him immune from attacks by his Christian neighbours or his own family. Harald temporarily lost control of southern Denmark when the Daniverke was overrun in 974. He was then ousted by his son Svein Forkbeard, who seized control of the throne after returning rich with Danegelds won in England.

cease and desist, and gave them accommodation to overwinter in Southampton. This suited the Vikings well: wealth was what they wanted and neither Olaf nor Svein had any intention of invading England – at least, not yet. In 994, no part of England was still under Viking rule. The Danelaw had

collapsed in 954, when Alfred the Great's descendants had expelled Eirik the Bloodaxe and replaced him with the Anglo-Saxon King Eadred. With the Vikings gone, England entered a peaceful and prosperous period: the country became a carefully administered nation with an efficient tax system

and over 70 mints producing a national currency of silver coins.

The creation of English coins came just in time for the Vikings. From 965, the great rivers of silver dirhams that had traditionally flowed into Scandinavia from the east dried up. The Arab mines had simply run out of silver and any

left over was blocked in transit by the Rus prince Svyatoslav's conflicts along the Russian rivers. The lack of income from the east was problematic for the Viking leaders trying to consolidate their powerbases at home. Svein Forkbeard was the reigning king of Denmark and Olaf Tryggvason aspired to unite Norway under his rule: both positions were expensive. In place of dirhams, the simplest source of revenue was just across the North Sea – England.

During the winter that Olaf Tryggvason and Svein Forkbeard spent in Southampton courtesy of King Æthelred, something curious occurred: Olaf converted to Christianity. At his baptism, attended by the Bishop of Winchester and King Æthelred,

Olaf promised to leave England and never return. The unlikely alliance between the Danish and Norwegian Vikings therefore ended, as Olaf sailed home. Olaf's plan was to use his vast hoard of Danegelds to seize power in Norway, and possibly beyond. Svein, fearing the potential repercussions of this for Denmark, followed Olaf soon afterwards. Æthelred had finally

Above: The newly converted Olaf Tryggvason is depicted with a retinue of Christian priests. Olaf proceeded with the often violent conversion of Norway after returning from England.

Left: An Anglo-Saxon coin from the time of Æthelred the Unready, now in the British Museum.

Above: The Battle of Svolder pitted Olaf Tryggvason against an alliance led by Svein Forkbeard and was fought out on the decks of lashed-together longships.

managed to see off England's attackers – for now.

Jarl Haakon of Hladir was the *de facto* ruler of Norway when Olaf returned from England, but his throat was slit by his own thrall not long afterwards. Olaf was pronounced king at the Gula Thing in 996 and immediately set about trying to convert the country to Christianity, forcing many regional jarls to be baptized under threat of violence. Olaf then began hostilities against his old raiding partner, Svein Forkbeard. Olaf claimed Svein owed him the island

of Zealand as a dowry payment for the marriage to his sister Thyri, and sailed to the southern Baltic to strengthen his ties there. This was to prove a fatal error, as an alliance of Svein, the Danish jarl Olof Skötkonung and the Norwegian jarl Eirik Hákonarson ambushed Olaf's fleet at Svolder on the Baltic Island of Rügen.

The Battle of Svolder

According to the sagas, Olaf's fleet was outnumbered at Svolder by 11 ships to 71. But instead of fleeing, the king decided to face the Danish ambushers, remarking: "The forest goats will not overcome us, for the Danes have the courage of goats. We will not fear that force because the Danes have never carried off the victory if they fought on ships."

Olaf then ordered his ships be lashed together to form a floating fort. From here, Olaf and his men were able to create barricades with oars and shields and rain down arrows and javelins upon the approaching ships. But then Olaf was aghast to see Eirik Haakonsson's ship, the *Iron Ram,* among the Danish fleet, because, as he told his crew, "they are Norwegians like us". Eirik used his ship to deadly effect, ramming it into the ships at the sides of Olaf's defensive fortress and then clearing their decks of warriors. The climax of the battle took place between two archers, Einar on Olaf's side and Fin on Eirik's:

> "Einar Tambarskelver, one of the sharpest of bowshooters, stood by the mast, and shot with his bow. Einar shot an arrow at Earl Eirik, which hit the tiller end just above the earl's head so hard that it entered the wood up to the arrow-shaft. The earl looked that way, and asked if they knew who had shot; and at the same moment another arrow flew between his hand and his side, and into the stuffing of the chief's stool, so that the barb stood far out on the other side. Then said the earl to a man called Fin... 'Shoot that tall man by the mast.' Fin shot; and the arrow hit the middle of Einar's bow just at the moment that Einar was drawing it, and the bow was split in two parts. 'What is that,' cried King Olaf, 'that broke with such a noise?' 'Norway, king, from thy hands,' cried Einar."
>
> – *Olaf's Saga,*
> translated by Samuel Laing

Above: A hoard of coins featuring the kings of England: Æthelred the Unready and Cnut the Great.

"The forest goats will not overcome us, for the Danes have the courage of goats."

— *Olaf Tryggvason*

St Brice's Day Massacre

Above: The St Brice's Day massacre ordered the ethnic cleansing of Scandinavian immigrants from English shores.

The St Brice's Day massacre is given only a passing mention in the *Anglo-Saxon Chronicle*, which reports:

> "…the king gave an order to slay all the Danes that were in England. This was accordingly done on the mass-day of St Brice; because it was told the king, that they would beshrew him of his life, and afterwards all his council, and then have his kingdom without any resistance."
>
> – *Anglo-Saxon Chronicle*, translated by Rev. James Ingram

The lurid detail of the slaughter, however, is provided by the monk John of Wallingford, whose entry about the events of the day serves as a black mark in the history book of Christian England:

> "… they agreed together that each province should kill the Danes at that time resident within its limits; and they appointed a certain day on which they should rise up against them. This was on the Saturday, on which (as has been before said) the Danes are in the habit of bathing; and, accordingly, at the set time they were destroyed most ruthlessly, from the least even to the greatest. They spared neither sex nor age, destroying together with them those women of their own nation who had consented to intermix with the Danes, and the children who had sprung from that foul adultery. Some women had their breasts cut off; others were buried alive in the ground; while the children were dashed to pieces against posts and stones. The Danes themselves were so utterly destroyed that there survived no one to tell what had been done, with the single exception of 12 young men, who escaped from the slaughter in London, and, fleeing to the Thames, threw themselves into a small boat, and, seizing the oars, quickly rowed themselves out of sight, and when they came to the sea-coast, they exchanged it for a ship, and spreading sail as quickly as they could set off for Denmark."
>
> – John of Wallingford, *The Chronicle of John of Wallingford*, translated by William Hunt

Olaf knew he had been defeated and, rather than face capture, he jumped into the sea in full battle gear and was never seen again. Although Olaf was made a saint, his kingdom was lost and the victors of Svolder divided up the country. It would take another 15 years for Norway to be united under a Norwegian king: Olaf Haraldsson.

In the meantime, the new co-ruler of Norway and King of Denmark, Svein Forkbeard, once again turned his attention to raiding England. This was bad news for King Æthelred, who had paid out tens of thousands in Danegelds during Svein's absence. Despite coins being specifically minted to buy off the Vikings, there was a limit to England's wealth. Desperate to turn the tide, Æthelred allied himself with his strong Norman neighbours by marrying the daughter of the Duke of Normandy, Emma. But all this did was to create difficult succession problems further down the line. Meanwhile the Viking attacks continued. In 1001, Æthelred was forced to pay 24,000 pounds (10,886kg) in Danegeld to a Viking force expelled from Norman shores, which had then harried the coast around Cornwall. The Danegelds were getting bigger and the time between raids shorter: Æthelred decided to take decisive action.

The king did so by issuing a royal decree that: "All the Danes who had sprung up in this island, sprouting like cockle amongst the wheat, were to be destroyed by a most just extermination." These were not the Vikings who

happened to be on English soil for a raid, but the Danes who had lived in England for generations. Despite being English citizens, these people dressed differently and talked differently, and that made them easy to pick out from the crowd on the day known as the St Brice's Day massacre.

Raids and Tribute

When the Danish men who escaped the St Brice's Day massacre reported to Svein Forkbeard's court, the king turned white with

Above: As Thorkell the Tall and Olaf Haraldsson pulled down London Bridge in 1009, King Æthelred attempted to protect England with prayers and penance.

Above: A fifteenth-century illustration of Svein Forkbeard disembarking from his flagship during the 1013 Viking invasion of England.

rage, not least because his sister was among those murdered. Worse news was to follow: the Anglo-Saxons in Oxford had chased the local Danes into a church and then burnt it to the ground when they could not get in, killing all who sought shelter there. There were also reports that some of the Danish victims had been flayed and their skins nailed to the doors of churches. In revenge, Svein ordered a new series of raids on England that took a no-holds-barred approach to excessive

violence. The result was an orgy of savagery that continued for over a decade and included the high-profile murder of the Bishop of Winchester – the man who had baptized Olaf Tryggvason – during a drunken dinner.

Svein was not the only Viking ordering raids against England. In 1009, a large army led by the Norwegian Viking Thorkell the Tall landed on English soil. At breaking point, the hapless King Æthelred did not send an army to meet Thorkell or raise a

Danegeld, but instead ordered a national programme of prayers and penance. This included a three-day fast, rolling masses and processions led by priests. Many sermons pointed the finger at the people of England, blaming the heathen peril on their sinful behaviour. But unsurprisingly the heightened Christan fervour did nothing to stem the Viking tide. Thorkell the Tall was soon joined by a new force led by Olaf Haraldsson, Norway's future king. Together, Olaf and Thorkell's men pulled down London Bridge from their longships with ropes and grappling hooks. The children's nursery rhyme *London Bridge is Falling Down* is thought to have stemmed from this event.

In 1012, after Olaf and Thorkell had spreads terror throughout England, Æthelred gave in. He offered the Vikings an unprecedented £48,000 pound Danegeld – a staggering sum that put a crippling hole in the royal coffers. From the 980s around 200,000 pounds (90,720kg) had been paid out to marauding Vikings, and England's mints could no longer keep up with the demand. By 1013 the country was on its knees.

This was the moment that Svein Forkbeard decided to strike. He assembled an invasion fleet and sailed for England with his 18-year-old son Cnut at his side. According to the *Encomium Emmae Reginae*, a history of Cnut commissioned by Æthelred's wife Emma, the ships were impressive:

"On one side lions moulded in gold were to be seen on the ships, on the other birds on the tops of the masts indicated by their movements the winds as they blew, or dragons of various kinds poured fire from their nostrils. Here there were glittering men of solid gold or silver nearly comparable to live ones."
– *Encomium Emmae Reginae*, translated by Alistair Campbell

KING CNUT

Svein landed in the north and quickly took the lands of the old Danelaw before moving his army south. Only in London was there any resistance to the invasion; it soon subsided. Æthelred fled his

---

"In this great expedition there was present no slave, no man freed from slavery, no low-born man, no man weakened by age."

— *Ecomium Emmae Reginae*

---

kingdom to his wife's homeland of Normandy and at the end of 1013 Svein Forkbeard was crowned King of England. It was to be a short reign: five weeks later Svein died and Æthelred sailed across the English Channel to reclaim his kingdom. Young and inexperienced, Cnut decided to renounce his claim to the English throne and return to Denmark. But in 1016 he was back, this time at the head of 200 ships and a vast army that included veterans like Thorkell the Tall. His campaign in many ways resembled his father's,

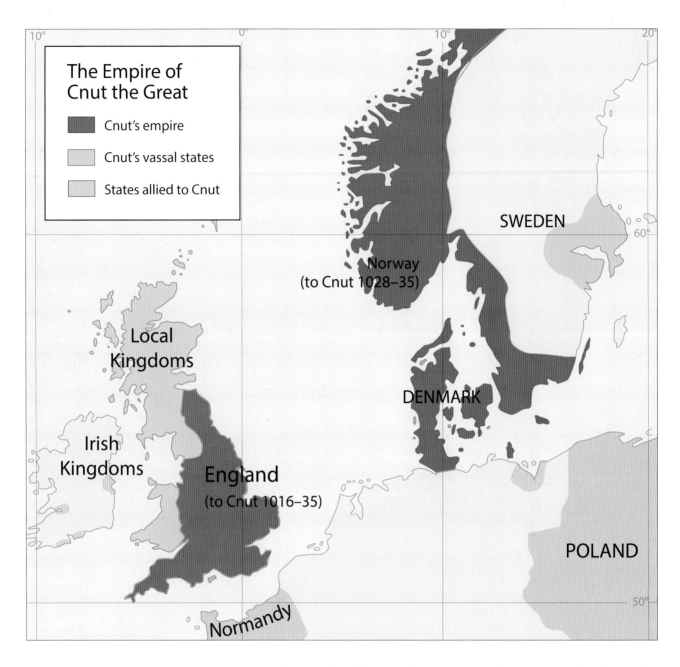

The Empire of
Cnut the Great

Cnut's empire

Cnut's vassal states

States allied to Cnut

10°   0°   10°   20°

SWEDEN
60°

Norway
(to Cnut 1028–35)

Local
Kingdoms

DENMARK

Irish
Kingdoms

England
(to Cnut 1016–35)

POLAND

50°

Normandy

Above: Cnut's reign lasted only two decades, but his accomplishments surpassed that of any of his Viking predecessors. By the time of his death, the Dane ruled over a North Sea Empire that included England, Norway, Denmark and part of Sweden, as shown on this map.

Facing page: Here, Cnut attempts to turn back the tide, an act intended to demonstrate that the king was only a man and not a god.

and is short in the telling. London was the seat of greatest resistance, and by the time Cnut reached the city, Æthelred had died. At the end of 1016, Cnut was crowned the new King of England.

Despite being known as Cnut the Great, or more commonly, Canute, the young king's reign lasted only two decades. Described as "the handsomest of men except for his nose which was thin, high set and rather hooked", Cnut is remembered as a just ruler who

restored peace to England, passed laws to protect the individual and married Æthelred's widow, Emma. However, Cnut is perhaps best known as the king who tried to stop the tide from coming into shore. According to English chronicler Henry of Huntington, Cnut ordered his throne be taken down to the seashore as the tide was coming in. There, in front of his royal retinue, Cnut told the water: "Thou art my subject, and this land on which I have set

> ## *"I therefore command thee come no further on to my land, and that thou presume not to wet the garments and limbs of thy king."*
>
> ### — Cnut

my chair is mine… I therefore command thee come no further on to my land, and that thou presume not to wet the garments and limbs of thy king."

Moments later, Cnut had wet feet and his royal court wondered whether their king had cracked. The story is often cast in a light

intended to show the folly of a king's hubris, but Cnut had the opposite intention. He wanted to prove that he was just a man, and that only God had the power to control the sea. After being soaked by the incoming tide, Cnut walked back to dry land and told the crowd that the power of a king was

empty and superficial next to that of God. He then hung his crown on a crucifix and never wore it again.

By the time of his death in 1035, Cnut had won what no other Viking had dared dream of: a North Sea empire that included England, Norway, Denmark and part of Sweden. But holding the threads of his empire together had proved difficult during Cnut's lifetime. Olaf Haraldsson, the raider who had pulled down London Bridge, proved to be a particular thorn in Cnut's side.

Olaf had seized the Norwegian throne in 1015 and had been busy reconverting the national population, many of whom had reverted back to paganism

Above: Olaf Haraldsson's fall at the Battle of Stiklestad only added to his legacy. After a year his body reportedly showed no signs of decay and he was canonized soon afterwards.

following Olaf Tryggvason's death. Olaf Haraldsson's missionary methods were simple: he travelled around the country building churches, destroying pagan shrines, rewarding those who agreed to be baptized and punishing those who didn't. His punishments included burning people alive, putting out their eyes or simply killing them where they stood. Olaf then allied himself to the Swedish King Olof Skötkonung by marrying his daughter, and together the two

kings began to harry the Danish coastline. Cnut reacted by sending a fleet of ships to confront Olaf in 1028, and all but wiped out the Norwegian's forces at a sea battle near the settlement of Skåne.

The defeated Olaf fled for Kievan Rus, which was then under the control of Yaroslav, son of Vladimir. Here, Olaf was able to raise a small force to try to take back Norway. His ranks were swelled as he travelled through Sweden towards the fated

battle-site of Stiklestad, around 72km (45 miles) northeast of Trondheim, Norway. With Olaf was his 15-year-old brother Harald Sigurdsson, later to be known as Harald Hardrada, or "Hard Ruler", who pleaded to be allowed to join the battle against King Cnut. When Olaf demurred, Harald insisted by saying that if he was too weak to grasp a sword, he would strap its hilt to his hand instead.

Although the 1030 Battle of Stiklestad is one of the most famous in Norwegian history, there is little to tell about the day. Olaf's newly converted warriors led the front line with the rallying cry "Forward Christ-men, forward cross-men, forward king's men". However, their courage and faith could not prevent a crushing defeat. Olaf's army only numbered around 4000 warriors, less than a quarter of Cnut's formidable force, which happened to be the largest army ever assembled on Scandinavian

Above: The 1030 Battle of Stiklestad is one of the most famous in Norwegian history, despite it taking little more than a hour to complete.

Above: A copper panel from Tamdrup Church in Jutland, Denmark, showing King Harald Bluetooth's baptism by the cleric Poppa.

soil. Within an hour, Olaf's army had been overwhelmed and their king felled. Olaf's loyal bodyguard surrounded their king and fought to the last, but the day had been lost.

Also cut down was Olaf's half-brother Harald, although he had enough strength to drag himself to a nearby forest for shelter. Here, he was taken in by a farmer and his wife who nursed him back to health. The body of Olaf, meanwhile, was stolen away from the battlefield and buried. One year on, Olaf's remains were exhumed and, according to the sagas, his

holy body showed no signs of decay. He was canonized soon afterwards.

THE LAST VIKING

When Harald regained his strength, he made the perilous journey over the Norwegian mountains into Sweden. From there he followed his brother's route to Russia, where he became the honoured guest of Yaroslav. Unlike his father Vladimir, Yaroslav was not dismissive of his Scandinavian heritage; he had married a Swedish princess, regularly sent Vikings to join the Byzantine emperor's

Varangian Guard in Constantinople and now took the teenage Harald under his wing.

There was good reason for Harald to have his own eponymous saga. Described as a "handsome man, of noble appearance; his hair and beard yellow", Harald's exploits in the east alone are enough to fill several volumes. In this way, Harald represents the late, great warrior of the Viking age – his heroism and daring are matched only by his cunning and double-dealing, the prerequisites of any warrior who has left the Scandinavian homelands to go "a Viking" abroad.

Yaroslav clearly recognized Harald's calling as a leader of men, and spent three years schooling him in the art of warfare. He was given command of over 500 warriors and put on military campaigns everywhere from Staraya Ladoga in the north to Kiev in the south. Then, Yaroslav dispatched Harald to Miklagarðr – the great city of Constantinople – where he became part of the Byzantine emperor's Varangian Guard. This was where Harald was able to hone his fighting craft, and there are many episodes in his saga celebrating his ruthless ability as a Varangian commander.

These episodes include Harald's capture of a castle in Sicily by attaching splinters of wood and tar to small birds that nested there and setting them alight. The returning birds then set their nests and the fortress ablaze, opening the way for its capture. Harald was reported to have taken another city by pretending to be dead and then leaping from his coffin once

inside the city gates. Harald's campaigns with the Varangian Guard took him to Greece, and east to Jerusalem and the Arabic "Serkland", where he "took 80 cities of the Moors". Later, Harald was charged with blinding the unpopular Byzantine Emperor Michael V by gouging out his eyes, a task he took upon himself to complete.

After 10 years abroad, Harald decided to travel home to reclaim his half-brother Olaf's throne in Norway. Now married to Yaroslav's daughter Ellisif and accompanied by a large bodyguard of battle-hardened Varangians, Harald sailed west into the Baltic

> *"[Harald] was stern and severe to his enemies, and avenged cruelly all opposition or misdeed."*
>
> — *Snorri Sturluson*

aboard ships laden heavy with his booty accumulated in the east. When he reached Norway in 1045, Harald found things had greatly changed. Cnut had died in 1035, and after a confusing succession of leaders, Olaf Haraldson's illegitimate son Magnus the Good was crowned King of Norway and Denmark, with a regent, Svein Ulfsson, in charge of Denmark. On Harald's arrival home, Magnus agreed to give half of Norway to his uncle in exchange for half of his Varangian loot: but then Magnus died, making Harald the sole ruler. On hearing this

Above: A statue of Yaroslav the Wise, the Rus prince who took Harald Hardrada under his wing following the Battle of Stiklestad.

news, Svein Ulfsson immediately crowned himself king of Denmark and in doing so turned Harald into a bitter enemy.

For nearly two decades, Harald engaged in a relentless and ultimately futile campaign of raids along the Danish coast. One noteworthy result was the building of the blockade of the Skuldelev channel in Denmark's Roskilde Fjord on the island of Zealand. Olaf Haraldson's *Long Serpent* may have been one of the longships sunk in the channel to prevent a sea attack by Harald Hardrada. It worked, and the settlement of Roskilde survived unharmed. Denmark's Hedeby was not so lucky: Harald attacked the trading town and razed it to the ground. It was an utterly pointless act that summed up his campaign against Svein. In 1064, the two kings met and agreed to a truce: Svein would keep Denmark and Harald Norway.

THE END OF THE VIKINGS

Harald's destiny, in the end, was bound to that of two other kings whose veins also ran with Viking blood: Harold Godwinsson of England and William of Normandy, or William the Conqueror as he became known. All three wanted the English throne and their ambitions would be played out in a bloody finale that left only one of them standing. Their fate would mark the end of the Viking Age in the very land where the first Scandinavian raiders arrived nearly three centuries earlier.

Normandy had been gifted to the Viking raider Rollo in the

tenth century by the Frankish King Charles the Simple. William was Rollo's descendant, and had endured a troubled reign since inheriting the duchy at the age of seven. However, by the time he was an adult, William had secured the borders of Normandy through political alliance and had also bailed Harold Godwinson out of hot water when he was captured and imprisoned on French soil. This began something of a relationship between the two, with William knighting Harold and putting him up as an honoured guest in Normandy. According to some sources, Harold promised to support William's claim to the English throne when the time came. William's claim was tenuous at best, and stemmed from the marriage of his great aunt Emma to King Æthelred the Unready.

However, Harold Godwinsson also felt he had a claim to the throne. He was married to the sister of the current king, Edward the Confessor, and considered himself the leading nobleman of England. Harold Godwinsson and his brother Tostig were the sons of the Dane Gytha Thorkelsdóttir and Godwin, the Earl of Wessex, a powerful man at the court of King Cnut. In 1042, it was Godwin that secured Edward the Confessor's place on the throne, although their relationship afterwards was fraught. Edward sent Godwin into exile for refusing to put down rebels who had attacked Norman

Above: An illustration of Harold Godwinsson proclaiming his loyalty to William of Normandy. If such a pledge was indeed made, it had little impact on the events that followed.

Above: A scene from the Bayeux Tapestry shows Edward the Confessor meeting with Harold Godwinsson after his return from Normandy.

courtiers within his territory. A year later Godwin was back, and although his political pull was stronger than ever, he died soon afterwards. Godwin's son Harold took over where he had left off. Harold installed his brother Tostig as Earl of Northumbria and set about making himself the main power behind Edward's throne. When the childless Edward died in 1066, Harold Godwinsson pronounced himself the King of England the following day. Many remarked he had been king in all but name for the last decade, but Harold's official reign would be a mere nine months long.

Back in Oslo, Harald Hardrada, or "The Thunderbolt from the North" as he became known, was visited by none other than Tostig, Earl of Nothumbria. Harald had been too busy harrying Denmark to seriously consider invading England, but now the idea had a certain appeal. In a twisted piece of logic, Harald felt he had a legitimate claim to the throne through his nephew Magnus the Good. Magnus had had a treaty with King Cnut's son Harthacnut to inherit Denmark and England upon the king's death. As promised, Magnus had been given Norway, but had been too busy to bother with England; now, his uncle Harald felt he had a legitimate right to take it. Tostig, who was disgruntled with his brother Harold, was happy to provide a soothing voice of reason and agreement for Harald. Now, with the two allied and preparing their ships for war, the stage for a last Viking invasion was set.

The Battles of 1066

The two great battles for England – Stamford Bridge and Hastings – began with the threat of an invasion by William of Normandy. It was this that preoccupied Harold of England, as Harald Hardrada secretly readied his fleet of 200 ships to sail across the North Sea. As agreed, Harald's ally Tostig began a series of raids along England's southern coast and then headed north for the rendezvous point in the northeast. Unaware of his brother's plans, Harold marched his army south, fearing Tostig's raids may have been connected with an early Norman landing party. As Harold's men spent weeks watching uneasily across the sea for enemy ships, the *Anglo-Saxon Chronicle* recorded an omen in the night sky: "over all England such a portent as no man ever saw before." Unbeknown to Harold, this was Halley's Comet, making its 76-yearly appearance; instead, the king told his soldiers it was a sign he would defeat the Normans. The Normans, however, did not come. After a summer waiting, running down supplies and watching his men's morale fall, Harold had little choice but to stand his army down.

This was the moment when the invaders arrived, although they did not land on England's southern beaches but instead on its northeastern coast. It was at the mouth of the Humber River that Tostig met Harald, who was at the head of a fleet of 200 ships that carried an army of between 9000 and 12,000 warriors. After sailing up the Humber, Harald cut through all opposition on his way to the one-time capital of the Danelaw, York. Harald was confident enough not to leave a garrison at York and instead marched his army 11km (seven miles) east to Stamford Bridge on the River Derwent. Here, his men took off their battle armour and rested in the warm autumn sun. It was a costly mistake: before the Vikings knew it, Harold Godwinsson was upon them. After hearing of the Viking landing, Harold had reassembled his army

> *Harald had been too busy harrying Denmark to seriously consider invading England, but now the idea had a certain appeal.*

and marched it the 322km (200 miles) from London to York in an extraordinary five days. Now, as Harald looked up from his resting place he noticed an ominous sign in the distance, according to *Harald's Saga*: "A great army seemed coming against them, and they saw a cloud of dust as from horses' feet, and under it shining shields and bright armour".

Harald and his men struggled into their battle gear as a giant Viking brandishing an axe held the bridge against the Anglo-Saxon charge. According to legend, this guard only renounced his post after being undone by an upward spear thrust from below the bridge. As this was going on, Harald's men formed a shield wall over half a mile long with the king

Above: As the Anglo-Saxon and Viking armies faced each other, Harald and Tostig rode forward to parley with Harold in this classically-styled rendering.

Facing page: A map showing the advance of Harold's army against Harald and Tostig at the Battle of Stamford Bridge, 25 September 1066. The Viking reinforcements led by Oystein Orre came too late to save the day.

"That was but a little man, yet he sat firmly in his stirrups."

— Harald Hardrada

and his standard "Landwaster" at its centre. But there had been a bad omen when Harald had unsuccessfully tried to mount his horse, and been thrown. Observing this humiliation, Harold remarked: "What a great man, and of formidable appearance is he; but I think his luck has left him."

As the two armies faced each other, riders were dispatched to the front lines to parley. Harold was ready to offer terms to his brother Tostig – all the land that he could want in Northumbria in exchange for a truce. Tostig asked what

land would be offered to Harald, to which he received an icy reply: "Seven feet of English ground, or as much more as he may be taller than other men." Harald then asked Tostig to identify the man who had "spoken so well" and was told it was Harold Godwinsson himself. "That was but a little man, yet he sat firmly in his stirrups", Harald observed.

With this, battle commenced. Harold's main concern was trying to break through the Viking shield wall, but after cavalry charges and volleys of arrows and javelins, the

wall stood fast. Then, finally, the Vikings faltered and their shield wall trembled. Harald reportedly fell into a berserker fury:

"Now when King Harald Sigurdson saw this, he went into the fray where the greatest crash of weapons was, and there was a sharp conflict, in which many people fell on both sides. King Harald then was in a rage, and ran out in front of the array, and hewed down with both hands; so that neither helmet nor armour could withstand him, and all who were nearest gave way before him. It was then very near with the English that they had taken to flight."

– *Saga of Harald Hardrada*, translated by Samuel Laing

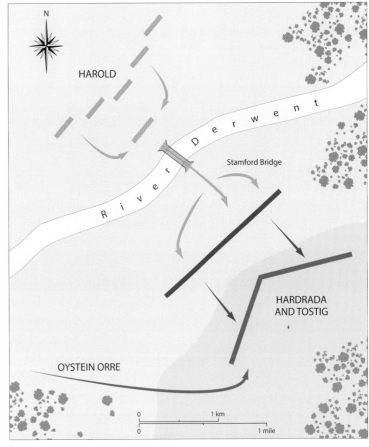

Above: King Harald Hardrada is fatally struck in the throat by an arrow and the day for the Vikings at Stamford Bridge is lost, in this painting by Norwegian Peter Nicolai Arbo.

Facing page: This fragment from the Bayeaux Tapestry shows the Norman cavalry struggling to break down the English shield wall. Note that the English defenders are armed with the two-handed axe, a common weapon among the English Huscarls.

> *"King Harald then was in a rage,*
> *and ran out in front of the array,*
> *and hewed down with both hands."*
>
> — *Saga of Harald Hardrada*

Just as it looked as if Harald had single-handedly turned the tide of the battle, he was struck in the windpipe by an arrow and killed. Shortly afterwards, Tostig was also slain. By the time Viking reinforcements had made their way the 18km (11 miles) from their docked fleet, the day was lost. During the vast Viking retreat to the coast, most of the warriors were hewn down or otherwise drowned trying to swim to their ships. There were so few survivors left that only 24 ships were needed to take them home. The remains of the last great Viking, Harald Hardrada, would be sent home to Norway nearly a year later. His body was the only one: the thousands of Vikings killed at Stamford Bridge were left to rot on the battlefield; it was said their bones were still visible over a century later.

Enter the Normans

Harold Godwinsson had little time to rest his troops before news reached him of the Norman landing at Pevensey, East Sussex. His beleaguered army was certainly not at full strength when it reached London, and there were reports of many desertions along the way. After spending a frantic five days raising fresh men and supplies, Harold marched south to meet William's army head-on. Harold's force was thought to number around 7000 men, smaller than William's army of around 10,000 men, which included a cavalry and large contingent of archers. The soldiers of both sides donned the traditional battle gear of the time: chainmail coats, shields and conical helmets with nosepieces, and they carried spears, javelins and swords. Harold's men were

also armed with the battle-axes so beloved by the Viking warriors. Legend has it that William wore in his clothes the relic upon which Harold was said to swear an oath to uphold his claim to the throne. Both men felt they were Edward's legitimate successor, but only one

would wear the English crown at the day's end.

Harold's army took up its position at 9.00 AM on Saturday 14 October 1066, along the top of a ridge at the present-day Battle Abbey, 11km (seven miles) north of Hastings. The high ground gave

Above: The Anglo-Saxon shield wall endures another assault by the Norman cavalry in this painting of the Battle of Hastings by American artist Tom Lovell.

Above: A detail from the Bayeux Tapestry records the battle dress worn at Hastings: chainmail coats, kite shields and conical helmets with nosepieces.

the English king the advantage and he ordered his men to form a long shield wall. This meant William's men had to traverse up the slope in full battle gear to attack the ridge. Luckily for the Normans the ground was not particularly wet, and their archers immediately set about sending volleys of arrows from the bottom of the slope. Trumpets then heralded the Norman cavalry and infantry charges, but these broke harmlessly against the defenders' shield wall.

William twice tried to lure some of Harold's men from the ridge by feigning a Norman withdrawal. Although this achieved some success, Harold's line held solid. The day looked to favour the Anglo-Saxons when

a rumour went up that William was dead. To prove he was not, the Norman leader removed his helmet and galloped back and forth along his own line. As the afternoon drew on, William ordered a final and fatal assault on the ridge. William's men battered Harold's front line, as more arrow volleys from the back line thinned out those in the Anglo-Saxon shield wall.

Then, suddenly, all was lost. King Harold was struck down, and with his death came the Norman rout of the English. As the news went up that their king was dead, Harold's men fell into disarray. Those soldiers trying to flee the battlefield were hacked down in their thousands as the daylight

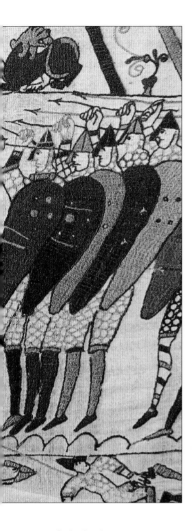

Above: The death of Harold at the Battle of Hastings. In reality, there is no indisputable proof that the Anglo-Saxon king was killed by an arrow to the eye.

faded. The Anglo-Saxon bodies were left where they fell, as William's victorious army counted its dead and buried them in mass graves.

Defeat and Conquest

So it was that William, the descendant of the Vikings, achieved what Harald and his Norwegian Vikings could not – the conquest of England. It was the last triumph of the Viking Age and arguably the greatest; there would not be another invasion of England. But while Scandinavian blood may have coursed through William's veins, he considered himself a Norman, not a Viking. And as he set about building a new kingdom, it would not be long before William's descendants called themselves "English": a people that even in the Medieval Age were bred from a centuries'-old genetic melting pot that included ancient Britons, Celts, Romans, Anglo-Saxons, Jutes, Picts, Normans, Vikings and others.

For the Scandinavian Vikings left over from the tumultuous events of 1066, change was on the horizon. The battered warriors who limped home from Harald's failed invasion would join their countrymen for a new period of history under the Christian nation states of Norway, Denmark and Sweden. And with this dawning of a new, modern Scandinavia, the Viking Age came to a close.

Conclusion

The year 1066 serves as a convenient end-point for the Viking Age, but Viking raids did not come to such an abrupt halt. In 1069, Danish King Svein Estridsson launched an invasion fleet to England with the aim of continuing where Harald Hardrada had left off. Together with a pretender to the throne, Edgar the Ætheling, Svein attacked the new Norman outposts and fomented uprisings among the local Anglo-Saxons.

William's crown looked momentarily under threat: large parts of Northumbria rose up in revolt and the city of York was overwhelmed by the Viking army. But Svein and Edgar had not planned an organized strategy against the Normans, and their victory was fleeting. Svein himself did not have the stomach for a drawn-out war and William paid him handsomely to sail home. It was the last case of an English Danegeld. Those Anglo-Saxons who had rebelled against William fared rather worse. In William's "Harrying of the North" his army burnt crops, livestock and homes, and slaughtered men, women and children; thousands died in the famines that followed.

Pagan Seaborne Raiders

William's mass murder of helpless Anglo-Saxon peasants reminds us that the Vikings were not the only Medieval Europeans capable of wanton violence and destruction. Æthelred's St Brice's Day massacre was ethnic cleansing on a nation-wide scale; the English king himself described it as "a most just extermination". In France, prince Lothar ravaged his own kingdom following the

Previous page - main image: The ruins of the Jarlshof settlement on the Shetland Islands. Jarlshof contains the most intact remains of any Viking site in Britain.

Previous page - inset image: This pendant of a Viking horseman is one of many pieces of jewellery discovered in the once thriving trading town of Birka.

Below: The Gokstad Ship, on display at the Viking Ship Museum in Oslo, Norway. This ship was constructed in the normal clinker style with each strake overlapping the one below it. Longships often had a length-to-beam ratio of 7:1, making them fast and flexible craft capable of speeds of up to 15 knots.

death of his father, Louis the Pious. Lothar's army reportedly committed acts of "devastation, burning, sacrilege and blasphemy", and plundered local churches as it marched. European churches and monasteries had always been targets. Of 113 recorded attacks on monasteries in Ireland, 26 were carried out by Vikings; the other 87 were by the Irish themselves.

There were two things that made the Viking raids stand out among the rest: first, they were pagans; and second, their attacks came from the sea. It is this combination that prompted the bewildered and terrified accounts from monks who were otherwise seeking a life of spiritual solitude

on remote, rocky coastlines. For Christians, the Viking attacks were incomprehensible sacrilege – but the warriors themselves did not have the slightest understanding of monasteries, or the curious, defenceless men inhabiting them.

The terror was carried by the Viking longship: the most lethally efficient weapon of the Medieval era. The image of the sleek ship, sailing swiftly into shore laden with bearded warriors howling for blood, retains a dreadful fascination. But the raids were never the product of a coherent Viking policy; instead they belonged to the warrior ideology that promoted adventure, warfare and the forging of lasting reputations. The Vikings were great opportunists who often had no idea where they were sailing to or what they would find when they arrived. Instead, they would form a plan when they landed, based on whatever circumstances the local situation presented. This could mean a smash-and-grab raid, taking local inhabitants for ransom or slavery, or setting up a trading emporium. Later, the Viking raids extended to invasion, migration and settlement.

Svein Estridsson's 1069 attacks on England were a classic example of Viking improvisation. Svein departed Scandinavia with invasion in mind and the possibility of whipping the newly oppressed Anglo-Saxon inhabitants into a countrywide rebellion. When this proved too difficult, Svein was happy to be paid off with the same silver and gold his predecessors sought nearly 300 years earlier at Lindisfarne. With

Areas of Scandinavian settlement

Svein, however, the great Viking raiding tradition came to an end.

Raiding had brought a floodtide of wealth into the Viking homelands, which both encouraged and enabled their expansion overseas. Before the raids began, Scandinavia had been an insular, isolated society formed far away from wider view. At its peak a few centuries later, Viking influence stretched from America in the west to Constantinople in the east and the Mediterranean in the south. In this time, the Vikings had ruled over realms in Russia, Normandy and England; they had colonized Greenland, Iceland, the Faroe Islands, the Shetlands, Orkney and the Isle of Man; they had built settlements from Newfoundland to Kiev; and

Above: A map showing the areas where Viking raiders and their descendants commonly settled. The true scope of their influence is of course impossible to record, as generations of Vikings became assimilated into the local cultures of England and Normandy.

Facing page: A statue of the great Viking explorer Leif Eiriksson, the first European to discover America, stands outside the Hallgrímskirkja Church in Reykjavík, Iceland.

Viking blood flowed through the veins of Europeans everywhere as the warriors and their families became assimilated into native populations.

Christian Conversion

While the Vikings had burst suddenly and inexplicably onto the Medieval scene abroad, change also came fast to the Viking homelands. The small trading villages of Kaupang, Birka and Hedeby, which had given the Vikings early exposure to other people and cultures, quickly grew into thriving, cosmopolitan towns. Warriors returning from overseas raids brought stories about the strange new Christian faith; missionaries from the European continent travelled to Scandinavia to spread the word. Before long, Viking kings were renouncing their pagan ways and trying to unite Scandinavia into centralized, Christian kingdoms.

The Christian motivation was often more political than ideological: reigning under Christ gave Viking kings a divinely ordained right to rule; it also allied them with the other Christian kingdoms of Europe. Christianity, therefore, was a uniting force that offered greater power and control. Early Christian Scandinavians had lived alongside their pagan neighbours without trouble, but under the first Christian kings of Norway – Olaf Tryggvason and Olaf Haraldsson – there was little choice but to convert. Any Vikings who failed to renounce their pagan gods or refused to be baptized were mutilated, cut down or burned alive. Norway and Denmark became the

first Christian countries, followed by Sweden in the twelfth century: these were the new nation states of Scandinavia under God.

Christ was a difficult proposition for many pagan warriors. Under Thor and Odin they had been encouraged to seek adventure, combat and riches, and return with stories of their great exploits, or otherwise die in a blaze of glory. Their gods were like helpful friends who could lend a hand if the right sacrifice was provided. Death was not to be feared, as Odin would welcome all warriors into Valhöll as long as they died with honour. But the Christian god frowned on all of this. He was a strict and severe judge who expected his flock to live morally to earn their place in heaven – those who failed would suffer eternal damnation. To many Vikings, Christian morals were as alien as the plethora of rules that came with the new religion – rules on when to eat meat, rules that forbade spells and sacrifice, rules that outlawed all pagan gods.

Christianity, however, brought something else to its newly converted Viking brethren: a written language. And it was with this language that Scandinavians and Icelanders began writing down the great Viking stories and poems that had previously only been told through word of mouth. This new prose spared no violent detail or heroic flourish in its lavish retelling of the Viking warriors and their feats.

In historical terms, the Vikings came and went in a flash: they exploded brutally and brilliantly onto the world in the eighth

century and within a few centuries they were gone. Apart from their colonies in the North Atlantic, the Vikings were ousted from their settlements abroad or otherwise integrated into the native populace. There would be no lasting Viking Empire. However, through horrified reports written by their Christian victims, the

bewildered accounts of foreign travellers and the poems and sagas that celebrated their great deeds, the Vikings achieved the thing that was most important to them: a lasting legacy.

My mother wants a price paid
To purchase my
proud-oared ship

Standing high in the stern
I'll scour for plunder.
The stout Viking steersman
Of this shining vessel:
Then home to harbour
After hewing down a man
or two.

— *Egil's Saga*,
translated by Herman Pálsson
and Paul Edwards

Bibliography

Adam of Bremen, *History of Hamburg's Bishops* (CUP, 1959)

Auden, W.H., Taylor, P.B. (translators), *The Elder Edda: A Selection* (Random House, 1970)

Bessinger, Jess B., Creed, Robert P., *Franciplegius: Medieval and Linguistic Studies in Honor of Francis Peabody Magoun, Jr.* (New York University Press, 1965)

Bray, Olive (translator), *Poetic Edda* (Viking Club, 1908)

Brink, Stefan (editor), *The Viking World* (Routledge, 2008)

Campbell, Alistair (translator), *Ecomium Emmae Reginae* (CUP, 1998)

Collingwood, W.G., Stefansson, J., *The Life and Death of Cormac the Skald* (Holmes Ulverston, 1902)

Cross, S.H., Sherbowitz-Wetzor, O.P. (translators), *The Russian Primary Chronicle: Laurentian Text* (Medieval Academy of America, 2012)

Crossley-Holland, Kevin, *The Penguin Book of Norse Myths: Gods of the Vikings* (Penguin, 2011)

Dasent, George W. (translator), *The Story of Burnt Njal* (J.M. Dent & Sons Ltd, 1911)

Earle, John, *Anglo-Saxon Literature* (Tredition Classics, 2012)

Graham-Campbell, James, *The Viking World* (Frances Lincoln, 1980)

Grammaticus, Saxo, *The Danish History of Saxo Grammaticus* (Online Medieval & Classical Library)

Green, W.C. (translator), *Egil's Saga* (Digireads, 2011)

Haywood, John, *The Penguin Historical Atlas of the Vikings* (Penguin, 1995)

Hermes, Nizar F., *The [European] Other in Medieval Arabic Literature and Culture: Ninth–Twelfth Century AD* (Palgrave Macmillan, 2012)

Hervey, Francis (translator), *Corolla Sancti Eadmundi* (London, 1907)

Hodges, Richard, *Goodbye to the Vikings?: Re-Reading Early Medieval Archaeology* (Gerald Duckworth & Co., 2006)

Icelandic Sagas (Icelandic Saga Database)

Jones, Gwyn, *A History of the Vikings* (OUP, 1968)

Laxdæla Saga (Project Gutenberg eBook)

Lee, Sidney, *Dictionary of National Biography* (Smith, Elder & Co., 1897)

Lewis, Archibald R., *The Islamic World and the West, A.D. 622–1492* (John Wiley & Sons, 1971)

Logan, Donald F., *The Vikings in History* (Routledge, 2005)

Magnusson, Magnus, *Vikings!* (BCA, 1980)

Mango, Cyril (translator), *The Homilies of Photius, Patriarch of Constantinople* (Harvard University Press, 1958)

Marsden, John, *The Fury of the Northmen* (St Martins Press, 1995)

Page, R.I., *Chronicles of the Vikings* (The British Museum Press, 1995)

Parker, Philip, *The Northmen's Fury: A History of the Viking World* (Jonathan Cape, 2014)

Prosecky, Jiri, Charvat, Petr, *Ibrahim Ibn Ya'qub At-Turtushi* (Academy of Sciences of the Czech Republic, 1996)

Robinson, Charles H., *Anskar: The Apostle of the North* (SPCK, 1921)

Roesdahl, Else, *The Vikings* (Penguin, 1992)

Rhys, Ernest (translator), *The Anglo-Saxon Chronicle* (Dent, 1912)

Sawyer, Peter, *The Oxford Illustrated History of the Vikings* (OUP, 1997)

Seaver, Kirten, *The Last Vikings: The Epic Story of the Great Norse Voyagers* (I.B. Tauris, 2014)

Short, William R., *Viking Weapons and Combat Techniques* (Westholme, 2014)

Siddorn, J. Kim, *Viking Weapons and Warfare* (NPI Media Group, 2000)

Simeon of Durham, *The Historical Works of Simeon of Durham* (Nabu Press, 2014)

Skaldaspillir, Eyvindr, *Hákonarmál* (Online Medieval & Classical Library)

Snorri Sturlson, *Heimskringla* (Online Medieval & Classical Library)

Stevenson, W.H., *Asser's Life of King Alfred* (Clarendon Press, 1904)

Tierney, J.J. (translator), Dicuil, *Liber de Mensura Orbis Terrae* (London, 1967)

Todd, James H., *The War of the Irish Against the Foreigners* (Longmans, Green, Reader and Dyer, 1867)

Williams, Gareth, *The Viking Ship* (The British Museum, 2014)

Williams, Gareth (editor), *Vikings: Life and Legend* (The British Museum, 2014)

Wilson, David M., *The Viking Achievement* (BCA, 1974) Page

Index

GREENLAND

Baffin Island

H E L L U L A N D

Western Settlement ○

Eastern Settlement
○

Davis Strait

ICELAND

*Norwegia
Sea*

FAROE
ISLANDS

A T L A N T I C

O C E A N

KINGDOM
OF THE PICTS

*Nor
Se*

M
A
R
K
L
A
N
D

Labrador

L'Anse aux Meadows ○

IRISH
KINGDOMS

Dublin ○

York ○

Lincoln
○

ANGLO-SAXON
KINGDOMS

WELSH
KINGDOMS

London ○

A

V
I
N
L
A
N
D

Newfoundland

Seine

Loire

FRAN

LEON

NAVARRE
ARAGON

Oporto ○

MUSLIM
STATES

Barcelona
○

Tarragona ○

EMIRATE
OF CORDOBA

Cartagena ○